"It is a pleasure to read this subtle, contemporary exposition of a great Buddhist classic. Connelly's insightful and often-moving commentary displays the profound relevance of Vasubandhu's Yogacara philosophy both to personal practice and to the wider social world."

—Jonathan C. Gold, professor of religion, Princeton University, and author of *Paving the Great Way: Vasubandhu's Unifying Buddhist Philosophy*

"Ben Connelly's extraordinary new book is almost impossible to classify. Framed as a fresh translation of and commentary on the 'Treatise on Three Natures' by the great Indian Buddhist master Vasubandhu, it is that and very much more. It is also a memoir, a psychological study, an exploration of social and political concerns, and an exercise in interreligious inquiry. Beautifully written, it fuses lucid explanations of often-difficult Yogacara ideas with attention to everyday concerns in a way that can help all of us apply Buddhist wisdom to the lives we live in the twenty-first century. Through such a fusion, Connelly points the way toward a new and distinctive form of Buddhist commentary uniquely suited to our complex and contentious era."

—Roger R. Jackson, emeritus professor of religion, Carleton College, and author of *Mind Seeing Mind: Mahāmudrā and the Geluk Tradition of Tibetan Buddhism* and *Rebirth: A Guide to Mind, Karma, and Cosmos in the Buddhist World*

"The practical application of Vasubandhu's ancient wisdom to contemporary oppressive challenges is no small task, yet Ben Connelly, through his own wounded-healer imagination, lived experiences in diverse relationships, and appreciation for freedom fighters, shows us how to understand and embody the mystery of Vasubandhu's teachings without getting lost in esoterica and spiritual bypassing."

—Pamela Ayo Yetunde, co-editor, *Black and Buddhist: What Buddhism Can Teach Us About Race, Resilience, Transformation and Freedom*

"Connelly's commentary on Vasubandhu's 'Treatise on Three Natures' offers a rare and welcome combination of scholarship and insight born of deep study and practice. The goal of human flourishing and freedom from suffering is at the center of his exposition of every verse. Connelly offers the wisdom of Yogacara that is simultaneously a path of transformation."

—Anantanand Rambachan, emeritus professor of religion, Saint Olaf College, and author of *A Hindu Theology of Liberation: Not-Two is Not One*

"*Vasubandhu's 'Three Natures': A Practitioner's Guide for Liberation* is a remarkable book, a powerful and lucid exploration, and a beautiful new translation of the 'Treatise on Three Natures.' One of the great virtues of this important work by scholar and practitioner Ben Connelly is its focus on the practical application of the Yogacara view."

—Roshi Joan Halifax, founding abbot, Upaya Zen Center, and author of *Standing at the Edge: Finding Freedom Where Fear and Courage Meet*

"I am deeply delighted by Ben's contribution. This book is an enlightening example of applied Buddhism. Ben has integrated and innovated a rich weave of practice, scholarship, and contemporary issues. Offering wisdom based on the rich teachings of Vasubandhu on the three natures, this book is an inspiring model of the new face of Buddhism; it opens many doors to personal and social transformation, sorely needed. This is a wonderful read that made both my heart and mind sing with fresh, meaningful possibilities."

—Dr. Larry Ward, author of *America's Racial Karma: An Invitation to Heal*

VASUBANDHU'S "THREE NATURES"

A Practitioner's Guide for Liberation

Ben Connelly

With a new translation of Vasubandhu's
"Treatise on Three Natures" by
Ben Connelly and Weijen Teng

Wisdom

Wisdom Publications
199 Elm Street
Somerville, MA 02144 USA
wisdomexperience.org

Library of Congress Cataloging-in-Publication Data
Names: Connelly, Ben, author. | Teng, Weijen, translator.
Title: Vasubandhu's "Three natures": a practitioner's guide for liberation / Ben Connelly; with a new translation of Vasubandhu's "Treatise on Three Natures" by Ben Connelly and Weijen Teng.
Description: First edition. | Somerville: Wisdom Publications, 2022. | Includes bibliographical references and index.
Identifiers: LCCN 2022008259 (print) | LCCN 2022008260 (ebook) | ISBN 9781614297536 (paperback) | ISBN 9781614297697 (ebook)
Subjects: LCSH: Yogācāra (Buddhism) | Mādhyamika (Buddhism) | Buddhist philosophy. | Buddhism—Social aspects.
Classification: LCC BQ7494 .C66 2022 (print) | LCC BQ7494 (ebook) | DDC 294.3/92—dc23/eng/20220517
LC record available at https://lccn.loc.gov/2022008259
LC ebook record available at https://lccn.loc.gov/2022008260

ISBN 978-1-61429-753-6   ebook ISBN 978-1-61429-769-7

26 25 24 23 22   5 4 3 2 1

Cover design by Phil Pascuzzo. Interior design by Gopa & Ted 2. Typeset by James D. Skatges.

MIX
Paper from
responsible sources
FSC® C011935

Please visit fscus.org.

Contents

Introduction

Just now, I am writing and you are reading, or I imagine you to be reading, and you imagine me to be writing. We are imagining each other, and I feel happy thinking this is true. As I imagine, here on my porch, a young couple is walking by with their cat on a leash. It is election day in the United States. I just voted. Are you imagining too? As I imagine, I call into my heart the wish that you and all of us may be well, that we may heal all of our wounds, and be free from all that binds us, for I believe that we depend on each other, and I believe that how we imagine is inextricably bound to our shared capacity for liberation.

This book is a new translation and commentary on Vasubandhu's *Trisvabhavanirdesa* (in Tibetan, *Rang bzhin gsum nges par bstan pa*), or "Treatise on Three Natures." The purpose of this book is to help people understand a way of looking at things, a way of understanding the world, ourselves, and others, that was created to alleviate suffering and promote well-being. The treatise itself is challenging; the commentary is to bring its message down to earth, to bring the wisdom into our day-to-day lives and activities.

I teach this material because, in my experience, it works. Although the text and this book are rooted in the Buddhist tradition, they can be of benefit to people of any, or no, religion. They accord with what in the West we call *psychology* and *phenomenology*, and bear striking commonalities with elements of cognitive science and neuroscience. They do not require belief in things for which there is no evidence but acknowledge that such beliefs matter.

The teaching of the three natures—three interrelated aspects of experience—shows how imagination and awareness of interdependence can be harnessed to heal and transform systems of harm within ourselves and our communities, even as it affirms the radical message of Mahayana Buddhism, that our broken world is inseparable from wholeness and liberation.

The three natures provide an empowering model for understanding how we can practice freedom from harmful personal and family patterns, addiction, trauma, and systems of oppression; they show a path to personal and communal healing. They affirm agency, experience, and interdependence while relentlessly challenging tendencies to become prejudiced or stagnant. By radically affirming experience, constantly challenging our fixations, and emphasizing that each moment contributes to the well-being or suffering of the whole, these teachings help us find our own role in the path of liberation.

The Yogacara school of Buddhism, of which Vasubandhu was one of the founders, emphasizes that we experience our lives through the lens of our conditioning. I am a white bisexual man raised middle class in Iowa with the idea that love is pervasive but so are violence and oppression, and that we can take action to create a world of peace and justice. My way of expressing and understanding these ancient teachings is informed by my particular cultural environments, as well as my training as a Soto Zen priest. My engagement with them also emerges from the vision and inspiration of people from many different cultures and backgrounds, and I will seek to amplify their voices in this book. My first encounter with Buddhism was with a joyful Japanese Nichiren monk on a cross-country peace march, and the point at which I really turned my life toward Buddhist practice was when I read the words of Thich Nhat Hanh, whose Yogacara teachings of a path of Engaged Buddhism remains a constant touchstone.

I will write about the implications of these teachings for liberation from many causes of suffering. I believe upholding the Mahayana vow to practice for universal liberation by definition includes working to dismantle harmful systems in which we live.

Yogacara Buddhism arose somewhere between the first and third century CE, was codified by Asanga and Vasubandhu in the fourth and fifth centuries, and has gone on to have a deep influence on many Buddhist traditions to this day. Although the small Hosso school in Japan is the only contemporary Yogacara school, Yogacara ideas and practices permeate Buddhist cultures and teachings.

The three natures form the philosophical backbone of Yogacara. The imaginary, dependent, and complete, realized natures are inherent aspects of all phenomena. The imaginary nature of things is what we think they are. Their dependent nature is that they appear to arise from countless conditions. The complete, realized nature is that they already aren't things as we imagine them to be.

Vasubandhu, a Buddhist monk, lived sometime in the fourth and fifth centuries CE. The historical facts from this time are hazy. I will offer some commonly, but not universally, accepted aspects of his story. Early in life he was part of a school of Buddhism closely associated with what we now call Early Buddhism, akin to contemporary Theravada. As a writer he was prolific and influential. One of his early works, the *Abhidharmakosa*, has been the basic study text on Early Buddhist Abhidharma, essentially psychology, for many Tibetan and East Asian monks for over a thousand years. As his life went on, he became known as a key figure, along with his half-brother Asanga, in the Mahayana Yogacara tradition. In Tibetan Buddhism he is known as one of the Six Ornaments, the greatest Indian Buddhist teachers. In the Jodo Shinshu, Pure Land, tradition, he is known as one of the Seven Great Ancestors, and in Zen and Chan lineages he is known as the twenty-first ancestor.

Vasubandhu's influence and understanding of Buddhist thought is vast, but to me the most inspiring aspect is how his work evolved. Throughout his life he showed an unstinting willingness to challenge views he upheld before, to change and grow. The "Treatise on Three Natures" was one of his last works, and along with his "Thirty Verses on Consciousness Only," provides a compact summation of the wisdom of a life of inquiry.

Each chapter of this book begins with a verse from the *Trisvabhavanirdesa*, which is followed by commentary. The full text is included at the end of the book, in our English translation as well as romanized Sanskrit and Devanagari script. After you have read through a few chapters, I suggest you occasionally flip to the back and read through the whole treatise, or at least the section you are reading about, to keep a sense of its overall flow.

In our translation, Weijen Teng and I have tried to bring forth the meaning of the treatise in a way that will be most useful to Buddhist practitioners. The language of the root text in Sanskrit is poetic and playful. Having chosen meaning and readability as our primary concerns, we have not been able to bring out the playfulness as much as I'd like. Vasubandhu uses rhyme, repetition, and wordplay to subtle and complex effect. For instance, the second verse begins *yat khyati paratantro'sau yatha khyati sa kalpitaḥ*. A basic phonetic reading of this, with the repetition and jumble of *y*, *k*, and *t* sounds, may give you a sense of the music of the text. Verse 26 states *abhava-datathabhavat tadabhavasvabhavatah*. In this line Vasubandhu offers a kaleidoscopic array of three terms: the negative prefix *a-*; the word for existence, *bhava*; and the word for "this" or "thus," *tatha*. Meaning and sound roll and tumble over one another. This line has a complex philosophical message, which we'll investigate in chapter 26, and Vasubandhu delivers it in a line that sounds like it belongs in an Ella Fitzgerald scat solo. I have tried to bring a bit of this spirit to my commentary and hope it may infuse your practice.

One more note on the root text: at least twenty times Vasubandhu inserts words that essentially mean "it is said." I cannot stress enough the emphasis he places on the provisional nature of his teaching. Just as each Buddhist sutra begins "thus I have heard," he relentlessly acknowledges that right now we are involved in a cultural transmission, and that what he is offering is just words, not the ultimate truth.

* * *

bell hooks once wrote, "There must exist a paradigm, a practical model for social change that includes an understanding of ways to transform consciousness that are linked to efforts to transform structures." I once heard a talk by a climate scientist. He said he used to think that when people saw the data about the terrible impacts of climate change, they would take swift and decisive action to change course. He was saddened to see this was not the case and came to realize that what we need is not just scientific data, but a change of consciousness. Transformation of consciousness is the principal concern of Yogacara.

Although Vasubandhu's writings show common ground between the diverse belief systems of his time, the "Treatise on Three Natures" was written primarily for devoted Buddhist practitioners. Studying the text is meant to be a small part of an integrated path of healing and liberation. The *Dhammapada* says, "Dharma is not upheld by talking about it, Dharma is upheld by living in harmony with it."[1] Throughout this book I will refer to the practical implications of the text, but I'd also like to provide some practice context here before we begin.

The *Dhammapada* defines the path in simple terms: do no harm, cultivate the good, and train the mind. To delve more deeply, Yogacara texts say the cause and the result of liberation are the six *paramitas*, or perfections: generosity, ethical living, patience, energy, meditation, and wisdom. The three natures teachings are also rooted in the Early Buddhist eightfold path: holistic view, intention, speech, action, livelihood, effort, mindfulness, and meditation. If you practice these, this book will make more sense, and if you read this book, my hope is you will practice these more.

Here I'd like to emphasize two aspects of the Buddhist path: *vipassana* and *samatha,* insight and calm abiding. These terms are understood in various ways and encompass a broad array of practices. I present them here in practical terms rooted in Yogacara teachings.[2]

I invite you to practice vipassana through mindfulness of body, senses, and emotions. You can find excellent support for mindfulness practices in the *Satipatthana Sutta*, and from many Buddhist teachers, particularly those in the Theravada, Tibetan, and Insight traditions. To develop vipassana, I recommend that you devote energy every day to more deeply knowing the sensations of the body, and to what is seen, heard, smelled, and tasted. Feel your body in the chair, the breeze on your skin, see trees gently swaying, smell the rain touching the earth. This can be the basis for an ever-deepening sensitivity to your emotions. I am not talking about thinking about your feelings, or what you are feeling "about." I'm talking about simply naming and offering awareness to sorrow, joy, rage, jitteriness, torpor, bliss, shame, guilt, the whole array of emotions. I'm talking about seeing them come and go within a broad, compassionate field of awareness. You can develop this way of being in meditation, in dialogue, and in any moment of your day-to-day living. It is most powerful to integrate all these approaches through long-term practice.

In samatha, which in Yogacara can refer to objectless practice, there is no object we focus on, and no object we are trying to accomplish, nothing to attain. In Soto Zen this is our basic mode of meditation: *shikantaza*, just sitting. When meditating this is best employed when the "thinking" aspect of our experience is not dominating; if your mind is very busy, something calming, like focusing on the breath in the body, is good. Some Yogacara texts call such calming practices "access to samatha." If the mind is slowing down, if you have some awareness of the whole field of your experience—sights, sounds, smells, taste, body, and mind—then putting all practice down and simply resting in the naturalness of what's here is a powerful offering. We can bring objectlessness into day-to-day life by doing things with our whole being and putting down thoughts of an outcome. As Thich Nhat Hanh teaches, do the dishes just to do the dishes. As Shunryu Suzuki taught, sit with no gaining idea.

Yogacara teachings refer to two barriers: afflictive emotion and the delusion of separateness. They say Early Buddhist psychology and mindfulness practices are particularly powerful for healing the first, and

Mahayana teachings and objectless practice are most effective for liberation from the second. Early in the last millennium a Zen nun, Miaozhan, expressed her experience of the path:

> In the shade of two trees and the hanging green of
>   the cliffs
> One lamp for a thousand years broke open the
>   dark barriers
> I too now realize that phenomena are nothing but
>   a magic show
> And happily grow old among the mist, the rivers,
>   and the stones.[3]

We can bring joy, freedom, clarity, and direct engagement with what is here right now to our lives and our communities. We can, through practice, transform our relationship to and impact on our environment. We can bring these teachings through our way of being to our families, our habits of consumption, our jobs, our play, and our work for transforming the world. They can deepen the growing interest in mindfulness and meditation, so these may be a more powerful force for integrating personal and collective transformation.

We can bring the worldview of the three natures into every aspect of our lives. They are here to remind us of the root of Buddhist teachings: there is suffering in the world and we can do something about it. They will call us to understand that every person is always and able to manifest this liberative capacity only through the lenses of their current emotional, mental, and behavioral conditioning. They can help us meet people, including ourselves, where we are. They will call us to honor and find beneficial use of our capacity for imagination, to recognize ever more deeply that all things are interdependent, and to let into our hearts the fact that we are all always already inseparable from liberation.

1

Three Natures

The imaginary, dependent, and
Complete, realized natures:
The wise say these three
Are what is known as profound. ||1||

Here we enter together into a body of teaching formed from a central aspiration: that all beings everywhere throughout space and time be free from suffering. These teachings, like this aspiration, are challenging, paradoxical, and mind-bending, but they also point to the simple, natural experience of a compassion where no one and nothing is left out of the circle of care. To be wise, from a Yogacara perspective, is to know what we can offer in this moment that will be most beneficial, to know that all is interdependent, and to see and see through our delusions. Vasubandhu says this wisdom arises from deeply knowing these three aspects of things: their imaginary, dependent, and complete, realized natures.

The imaginary nature of things, *parikalpita svabhava*, is what you think they are and is sometimes also translated as the imputational, constructed, or fabricated nature. Their dependent nature, *paratantra svabhava*, is that they appear to manifest due to other conditions. Their complete, realized nature, *parinispanna svabhava,* is the truth that whatever appears isn't what it appears to be. These are intellectually challenging ideas, and it will take some time for them to make sense. However, once you begin to understand them, this intellectual challenge opens into a yet more profound, freeing, and mysterious challenge. This teaching is intended to crack through every hardened way of seeing things the mind and heart can make. It is to turn the mundane into the wondrous, the tiny into the vast, the infinite into the immediate, the known into the inconceivable, and anguish into joy, peace, and compassion.

Those of you familiar with other Buddhist teachings may see parallels between these three natures and teachings you already know. Studying the three natures can help to illuminate our understanding of all these related ideas and their real-life implications. The imaginary and complete, realized natures roughly correspond to common Buddhist dyads: samsara and nirvana, form and emptiness, conditioned and unconditioned, suffering and liberation, and relative and absolute. The dependent nature closely relates to the ideas of the twelvefold chain of dependent arising, interdependence, and inter-being. What much Mahayana literature calls "relative truth," Yogacara calls "imaginary." As we will see, this serves to make explicit the importance of karma, intentionality, in forming our experience. In simplest terms, it emphasizes why and how what we do matters.

Vasubandhu says we should deeply know these three natures, and that there is no way to enter their depths without study and investigation. Studying with the mind and with words is necessary, but meditation, ethical action, and a day-to-day return to the aspiration for liberation from suffering is the way to realize their true profundity. In the Yogacara approach to vipassana, or insight, we begin to know truth by listening to teachings. We know it more deeply through experiential investigation, and ultimately we know it by realizing that it is what we knew all along. I will encourage you throughout this book to study with your thinking mind, but also to study with your heart and your body—your eyes, ears, nose, and tongue. To taste the teachings, I hope you will test their truths against the truth of your own experience.

Every aspect of what we would conventionally call "experience" is of these three natures: sights, sounds, smells, tastes, physical sensations, thoughts, emotions, and our sense of being a self. For example, the cobalt blue car that I can see outside my window is of an imaginary nature. Whatever I am experiencing it to be right now (a memory, as I'm currently looking at letters on a screen), or now, as I turn my head to look at it again, is a construction of habits of consciousness and imagination. I suspect it will take some time for you to consider this a reasonable or useful claim, and so, dear reader, that's why I'm writing this book. That car is also of a dependent nature; countless conditions that are not the car create the appearance of a car: reflected sunlight, ocular nerves, supply chain software, oil refineries, the desire for wealth, and so on. This car is also of complete, realized nature; it isn't what I think it is. Recognizing that things aren't what you think they are can radically disarm the patterns of your mind that cause you to suffer and cause suffering. For example, in order to see the car in my normal way, I am usually ignorant of, or ignore, a vast array of conditions on which the appearance of the car depends—conditions that cause suffering in this time of climate crisis. These teachings are to help us move beyond this kind of ignorance.

The "knowledge" that white people are inherently superior to Black people and the "fact" that race exists as a biological truth were confirmed by nineteenth-century scientific experiments—which have since been disproven. This caused and causes incalculable harm. This "knowledge" is imaginary; it arises from conditions, and its complete, realized nature is that it is not real. And yet millions of people thought, and still think, it is true. Although many of us do not, the impacts of this view are pervasive: it affects where people live, the jobs we have, the wealth we inherit, our access to education, and so much more. They are alive in how I experience the world. This teaching is here so we may continually grow in our capacity to end and transform harmful patterns of which we are often unaware. By learning to see the three natures of the ideas that maintain harmful systems, we open the way for liberation.

The three natures can be misapplied—and easily misunderstood. Understanding the imaginary nature invites humility, not grandiosity. It affirms agency; it does not deny experiences. Understanding the dependent nature affirms kinship with all things; it does not deny differences or boundaries. Understanding the complete, realized nature brings faith, compassion, and joy; it does not deny suffering. The three natures provide medicine for our ongoing daily sufferings, no matter how small.

I was dreading the conversation. Why had my boss wanted to schedule a phone meeting? Why? I must have put my foot in it at our last committee meeting. I looked up to see the pale spring buds and realized that I'd walked for five minutes unaware, disembodied, absorbed in my churning mind. I imagined her stern face and fierce words. My face flushed with shame and anxiety. When she called, I took a deep breath to prepare as I answered the phone. Her voice was bright. In her careful way, she was calling to ask if I'd like to help with a new project. We parted with a laugh. The whole story of her judgment and anger that drove my anguish, so well developed and *so* real, was imaginary!

These types of situations are not uncommon, and they help us to see how much our imagination colors our life and drives our suffering. Saying that things have an imaginary nature is in part about disarming their power to drive us into the fires of desire, aversion, anger, and anxiety. However, Yogacara teachings, including the three natures, emphasize that things are imaginary for a paradoxical reason as well: to remind us that we always have power.

Yogacara teachings say that every cognitive, emotional, or behavioral action plants a seed that will bear a similar fruit in the future. Our experience in any moment is the fruit of past seeds that have been planted. Our response to what arises in each moment is what plants seeds for the future. What we conventionally think of as "experience" is what Yogacarins call the imaginary nature. If the seeds of past conditions create our imagination, our response is where we have power. We have the power to contribute to what will be imagined—that is to say, experienced—the power to plant seeds for future fruit.

This of course runs counter to most people's understanding, which is that our experience is of a consciousness observing an absolute physical reality.

Yogacara teachings sometimes acknowledge that there may be a reality "out there" that prompts experience. However, they say that since we know things only through the lens of our conditioning, we can't ultimately know anything outside of our perspective on it. It will take time to explore this radically challenging view, but for now, understand that this teaching is here to encourage you to focus on where you have the most power and agency: how you respond and act in each moment.

Each thing within experience is of dependent nature, as is the whole. Sometimes when I'm teaching, we play a little game. I point to an object and ask each person in the circle to name something on which the object depends. The brass bell depends on mining, hands, thoughts, childbirth, sex, food, dirt, sun, kindness, highways . . . It's fun at first, then it gets boring, and then we realize that we could go on forever if we had the will.

I remember when an understanding of this dependent nature landed in my heart. I was sitting on a therapist's couch and realized down to my bones that all the torment of my heart and mind, and all the cruel and harmful things I'd done, were dependent on suffering in my family and community. I saw how this suffering and harm tied me to countless generations of humanity. I felt profound grief, but with it, I felt my heart expand too. The space of a vast compassion for me and all my relations opened outward as I experienced the dependent nature of our suffering.

Because each thing is entirely dependent on all the other things, we can realize that, as Martin Luther King Jr. wrote in the "Letter from a Birmingham Jail," "we are caught in an inescapable network of mutuality . . . I cannot sit idly by." As we realize the dependent nature, our heart not only opens to the vastness of our connection within the web of the world's difficulties, but our bodies incline toward doing something that will heal. Realizing the dependent nature of things awakens not just compassion but also clarity about what will actually help. As we realize our interdependence, the illusion that avoidance, violence, and control are beneficial can fade away. We become more clear on what is the truly healing and liberative offering in each moment.

The complete, realized nature is the third aspect of what everything you are experiencing already is. The complete, realized nature is what the enlightened see, and what things actually are. The complete, realized nature is free from suffering and delusion. Tibetan Mahamudra texts sometimes say that we don't need to liberate the mind; we can just realize it is already liberated. Perhaps this seems a little mysterious. It will take time to explore Vasubandhu's teaching on this truth, but for now, I'd like to tell a brief story.

Last year I was offering a teaching at an Insight Meditation group in a glorious Unitarian church near Washington, DC. I was emphasizing what I believe to be the core of Early Buddhist teachings: that we each, at every moment, can offer something conducive to liberation from suffering. We can offer many things, and the best place to start is offering awareness of our bodies, our emotions, and what we are doing. Afterward a woman approached and told me she'd enjoyed the talk, but that as a Buddhist and a Lutheran, she was so happy to also have the idea of grace in her Lutheran life, and not just Buddhist practice. Her belief in God's grace gave her a sense that she was blessed by a wellness that came through no effort of her own. We had a nice connection, and she taught me that I had been missing something: I was upholding the Yogacara wisdom that because things are of an imaginary nature, we have the power to offer something beneficial, and that because they have dependent nature this offering is always collective. However, I was failing to convey the grace of the complete, realized nature. This teaching says that everything is always already free from suffering. What you see is what buddhas see, and you cannot be separate from Buddha. Buddha is not a deity; the word means "awakened one." It means one who is awake to the truth and thus experiences no suffering. The truth is already true, and we are already awake. We don't have to wait or strive for liberation. This moment is complete and real, beyond all ideas, and freedom is here.

Whether this seems true to you or not in this moment, I invite you to enter this study with a heart of trust. Trust that the process of study may open our hearts a little wider, may open our eyes and ears to the wondrous mystery of the moment, and may help us find our feet where they are most needed for healing and liberation.

2

Experience, Imagination, and Interdependence

What appears is the dependent.
How it appears is the imaginary,
Since it is dependent on conditions,
And it exists as mere imagination. ||2||

It's hot here in Minnesota midsummer, and I feel the warmth of my skin and the sun, high and bright above faintly shimmering asphalt roofs. I hear the sound of a fan behind me and feel the soft rush of air across my neck. It whirs, it hums. The sound is constant, but there's variation if I listen. Why listen? It's just a fan, I know. Here Vasubandhu is telling me, yes, something appears, but not in the way that I think it does. The words "how it appears" in this verse do not refer to the causes of the appearance, but to what it seems to be.

I think I am hearing a sound, which is a fan. Vasubandhu would call each of those things—*I*, *think*, *hearing*, *sound*, and *fan*—imaginary, but each affirms that something is appearing right now. It is simply not possible to know all the conditions that produce any of these things. What we *can* know is their dependent nature, that what appears is merely an infinite dependentness. Vasubandhu talks more about knowing this experientially, beyond cognition, later. Though experiential knowing usually arises unbidden from a deep commitment to meditation and ethical living, "Treatise on Three Natures" offers an opportunity for developing awareness of the dependent nature by thinking about it.

Let's take a moment to analyze the conditions that produce the conviction I have that there is a sound that is a fan. Does this sound I'm hearing depend on the fan or on the air? Both, I suppose. From the perspective of physics, what I experience as sounds are waves of air particles, not the fan, per se. More accurately it is the impact of these particles on the timpani inside the ear. Sound is actually touch. What I call *sound* is the experience my mind makes when air particles make contact with my ear (unless it's an old song stuck in my head with no apparent external source). So, dependent on millions of air particles and the conversion of touch on the timpani in the ear into a sensation of sound by my mind, I think there is a fan.

Next, I might analyze the conditions upon which each of the air particles depends and then move on to analyze each of the cilia in my ear, the fan, my brain, and then the electrical grid, and then perhaps the wind power advocates who've helped make it so the power from this house comes from wind turbines. It appears to me to be a sound, or a fan, or air particles on the ear, or brain processes, or wind turbines, or, or, or . . . But ultimately, these are just ideas. I haven't gotten closer to knowing what the sound or the fan *actually are*. "Sound" and "fan" like all these points of analysis are just descriptions, imputations, ways of thinking about things. They are creations of mind, imaginary. Here's an old Zen story that illustrates this:

> Two monks were debating outside the monastery
> One said, the wind moves,
> The other said, the flag moves,
> Sixth Ancestor Huineng said, not the wind, not the
>   flag, mind moves.

Writing this, I'm just creating different descriptions, "mind moves," things of imaginary nature. My mind does a lot of moving. This is one of the reasons I get up in the morning and meditate for an hour. I let the mind settle to see the "mind moves" and to be aware. Different descriptions are helpful, though. When people are stuck on their descriptions, it creates a lot of trouble. We need difference. "Mind moves" can help us let go of how stuck we are. Poetry or wise speech can sometimes shift us off the stable base of our assumptions and into something more free, more mysterious. Audre Lorde taught that creativity and difference are essential for liberation. She wrote, "it is out of Chaos that new worlds are born." Dependent on infinite conditions, something unknowable appears.

Realizing that what we experience is of an imaginary nature arising from conditions can help us to see just how wonderful and valuable the imagination is. When I hear the neighborhood children playing in the back yard, they shout out their shared imaginations in the present tense. "I'm getting in the rocket ship!" "Don't forget the baby!" As they dive into imagining, I hear them raising wave after wave of creativity and joy. Their tears and anger may come when they stop imagining—or, from a Yogacara perspective, when they stop *realizing* they are imagining.

Adults imagine new things, too: "I'm going to go for a walk." "Our Zen center should start a climate justice group." "Perhaps the Earth is spherical, not flat." "I don't have to keep entering these crappy relationships." "I could quit drinking." We sometimes leap into creativity, new imaginings. We imagine poems, songs, paintings, imagine new shapes and movements of the body as we dance. We might say that an individual is creative or imaginative, or that an event prompts a spark, but the three natures say every one of these imaginations arise from incalculable conditions. They don't really come from a particular incident or person. I worked as a songwriter for many years, and I'm pretty sure I can't just sit down and decide that today I will write the best song I will ever write. We sit down to write, and something appears.

As I write this line right now, I know this sentence might be cut or kept in the book you are reading. Conditions come together and we create something we like, or perhaps something we don't like. We can learn to make our offering and be free in the results. When we realize the imaginary and dependent nature, we orient ourselves toward creating the conditions for a more joyous, a more compassionate, a more peaceful imagination, for a better world. Musicians, chemists, dancers, carpenters, and chefs practice. They create the conditions for their amazing creations. Buddhist teachings emphasize practice, creating the conditions for liberation and healing. When Dr. King said, "I have a dream," he was a visionary, he was imagining, but his imagining was never his alone. His dream is not realized, but the dreaming goes on. We are always in this imagination dependent on one another, and we can practice opening up to possibility.

All this imagination and here I am in the heat with the fan, the sound. It is hard to believe that the fan is of imaginary nature. A fan is a fan is a fan! That seems solid and true. I am not able, in this moment, to truly forget, or not know, that this sound is a fan, but I *can* know that it is imaginary, dependent on the processes of mind. Vasubandhu says that whatever something appears to be is imaginary; it exists as mere imagination. He is affirming the existence of everything you believe exists. Everything you suffer over, cling to, rejoice about, ignore—yes, all of it exists. It matters because it exists *as mere imagination*, because it seems so real.

Last night I found myself pushed onto a stage in an ill-fitting cloak. I slowly realized as I wended my way among the actors that I was in a production of *Waiting for Godot*. I found it stressful to be onstage with no lines, no direction, in front of a packed theater. I was dreaming, but the anxiety I felt as I peered into the dark auditorium was as real as it gets. I woke up hot, and I relaxed as the thought appeared, "Ha! It was merely a dream." In the humid air, the tangle of sheets, and the dim light of dawn, I heard the sound of a fan.

3

It's Not What You Think

The constant absence of
How it appears in what appears
Is known as the complete, realized nature,
Since it is never otherwise. ||3||

Since my father died, I sometimes have dreams in which he comes to me. I remember the first time; it was early in the time of grieving. As ever, he was bearded, and he was wearing chinos and a buttoned shirt and appeared from an amorphous dark void. As we neared to embrace, he vanished. I awoke in anguish. Not long after, I was reading my father's copy of Homer's *Odyssey* and found the passage where Odysseus descends to Hades to find his mother. When he goes to embrace her, his arms pass through her as though she's made of mist. More recently, I have had dreams where I can hold my father in my arms. It has been a joy. Some folks would say Odysseus actually went to Hades, or that my father (or his spirit, as some might say) has actually visited me. Vasubandhu's third verse best reflects what

I believe. The experience and the feelings that arose, are vivid, real, and important. Both not being able to embrace and then embracing my father really matter to me. Whatever I think was happening in that moment cannot be ultimately proven to be true. I cannot find it and realizing this and learning to trust it opens me up to a sense of completeness.

The complete, realized nature, *parinispanna svabhava*, like the imaginary and dependent natures, is already how things are. Some translators have called it "the perfected," "the consummate," "the ultimate." *Pari* carries the connotation of completeness, and *nispanna*, the connotation of realized, fulfilled, or accomplished. Embedded in the term there is a sense of wholeness, a sense of realness, and the sense of what is realized by the enlightened, what is seen by buddhas. Vasubandhu says in this verse that "it is never otherwise." There's never anything happening that isn't complete, whole, realized. You are not ever seeing something other than what buddhas see, never knowing something other than what buddhas know.

According to the texts we have inherited, the historical Buddha saw how things really are and thus spent the remaining forty years of his life wandering, begging for his food, taking time for retreat, and serving the community wherever he went with profound ease, compassion, and wisdom. The path of wellness, of deep joyful engagement with the world, opens up when we know the complete, realized nature. Rather than "knowing" things in our conventional way, we can know that all those conventional ways are imaginary, they are just "how it appears," which cannot ultimately be found or proved to be real amid this somethingness that is happening now, which Vasubandhu calls here "what appears." It is precisely the impossibility of finding an ultimate existence of anything in any moment that is the ultimate, the complete, realized nature.

Technically speaking, in this verse "how it appears" refers to the imaginary nature, and "what appears" refers to the dependent nature. To recap the previous verse: from conditions something appears but is not what it seems; we cannot ultimately find or prove that what it looks like to us is real. It is this very quality of unlocatability that is the complete, realized nature.

My life is profoundly transformed as I practice knowing more and more deeply that all the things I think are real are not. In the "Thirty Verses on Consciousness Only," Vasubandhu writes, "When there is nothing to grasp, there is no grasping." This line is about finding liberation from suffering not by letting go, but by realizing there is nothing to hold. When joined with knowing the imaginary and dependent natures, this teaching shows that there is nothing to grasp, what we do always matters, and what we do is always collective.

The phrase "it is never otherwise" is important here. The idea that complete realization is the basic nature of every moment of experience has created wonderful innovations in Buddhism. In thirteenth-century Japan, Shinran founded Jodo Shinshu and Dogen founded Soto Zen. Both monks were spurred to spiritual quests in part by the paradox that nirvana is inseparable from our visceral, suffering world. At the root of Jodo Shinshu are the words *nembutsu*, or *namu amida butsu*—taking refuge in Amidha Buddha. *Nembutsu* emerges from the vow and compassion of Amitabha Buddha, whose realization is that all is realization. Shinran taught that this recitation, and our whole lives, can be an expression of gratitude for the fact that everything is already of complete, realized nature. Dogen emphasized "practice-realization." For him, *zazen* (sitting Zen) is not meditation practice but is the embodiment of complete, realized awakening. The first line of his *Universal Recommendation for Zazen* (*Fukanzazengi*) says, "The way is originally perfect and all-pervading. How could it be contingent on practice and realization?"[4] Although their teachings are varied and complex, both of these monks built their teachings on the faith that awakening is already here.

Gandhi once wrote, "Faith is not something to grasp, it is a state to grow into." It may take practice to trust that that there is nothing to hold onto, no ground on which this all rests. Contemporary neuroscience can help us get a sense of what this verse calls "the constant absence of how it appears in what appears." It is well-documented that our senses experience things 50–200 milliseconds later than they actually happen, and that our mind compensates for the lag. The mind guesses where objects are now based on information our sense organs received a while back and by the conditioning of our minds. That guess is what we see as "reality." Studies have shown that people in the United States tend to see Black men as larger than they actually are and as armed when they are not. In conventional terms, these are things people "see" rather than what they "think." In Yogacara terms, seeing and thinking are interdependent. Dependent on racist messages that Black men are more dangerous than white men, people imagine things that are not real.

Science is based on observing phenomena and collecting measurable, repeatable results. It is a method of inquiry. Through various means, numerous preeminent scientists have arrived at the idea that what we see is not ultimately real. Francis Crick, who won the Nobel Prize for groundbreaking work in DNA research, once wrote, "seeing is an active, constructive process . . . in fact we have no direct knowledge of objects in the world." Stephen Hawking wrote, "Histories of the universe depend on what is being observed, contrary to the usual idea that the universe has a unique, observer-independent history." Nima Arkani-Hamed writes of theoretical physicists, "Almost all of us believe that spacetime doesn't exist."[5]

I do not claim that the quotes above somehow prove that Yogacara is correct or that all scientists agree. I cite them here to help soften our conditioned tendency to believe that what we see, or even *can* see, is absolutely real. I also cite them to counter the idea that Yogacara ignores what is obviously true and confirmed by science: that matter is absolutely real. Yogacara does not undermine science, it merely shows that science occurs as moments of conscious experience and cannot happen anywhere else. It affirms what makes science powerful—inquiry and openness to new ways of knowing.

As the Nobel Prize–winning physicist Erwin Schrödinger once wrote, "the reason why our sentient, percipient and thinking ego is met nowhere within our scientific world picture can easily be indicated in seven words: because it is itself that world picture. It is identical with the whole and therefore cannot be contained in it as a part of it."

4

Not Two

What appears there? Unreal imagination.
How does it appear? As being dual.
What is its nonexistence?
The essential nonduality there. ||4||

Nonduality, *advaya*, is the foundation of the three natures. Our consciousness presents us with a world made of dualities: self/other, good/evil, existence/nonexistence, birth/death, dark/light, here/there. These are simply ways of looking at things; they are not ultimately real. Even nonduality and duality are not ultimately real, separate things. Dualities are important. When I bring the blade of the knife down, I want to know that the carrot is not my finger. When I am speaking to my child, I want to know how to use kind rather than harsh speech. In community, I want to be mindful that men have more access to wealth, power, and safety than women. When I am in the throes of conflict, I want to know that I am me and that other folks have their own autonomy so I can practice good boundaries.

However, I also want to know that all these dual appearances, fingers and carrots, kindness and harshness, male and female, self and other, are not ultimate truths. They are ways of looking at things. These dualities are creations of mind, hence all the things which appear as dual are nonexistent. We are inextricably in this together. The word "essential" in this verse is a translation of *dharmata*, which you could also say is "truthness," or "realness"; sometimes it's translated as "ultimate reality." Vasubandhu is telling us that there is something real and true right here: the nonduality of anything that we perceive as dual.

Throughout this text, Vasubandhu is playful in his use of language. In our translation, we have emphasized conveying meaning clearly, but we were not able to focus on conveying playfulness. However, it shows up in this verse. In verses 2 and 3 Vasubandhu says *what appears* is the dependent nature and *how it appears* is the imaginary; here he says *what appears* is the imaginary and *how it appears* is as dual. As he begins to directly address duality as false, he takes a duality he created in verses 2 and 3 and turns it on its head. He begins to show here what he will repeat throughout the text—a tendency to create a duality and then invert, shift, or dismantle it. He invites you to become adept at working with dualities while realizing their falseness and limitations, and he models the freedom available to us when we can enter this flow.

In the earliest body of Buddhist teachings, the Pali Canon, we find the *Kaccanagotta Sutta*, which serves as the foundation for much Mahayana thought.

> Kaccanagotta asks, "What is right view?" Buddha answers, "This world, Kaccana, for the most part depends upon a duality—upon the idea of existence and the idea of nonexistence. But for one who sees the origin of the world as it really is with correct wisdom, there is no idea of nonexistence in regard to the world. And for one who sees the cessation of the world as it really is with correct wisdom, there is no idea of existence in regard to the world.[6]

The *Lankavatara Sutra* states:

> [One] who sees the world like this
> neither existing nor not existing
> nor both of these nor neither
> transforms their mind and finds no self.[7]

Right view is not having the idea of existence or nonexistence occur to you. Seeing the nonduality of existence and nonexistence is essential to ending suffering. When there is nothing to grasp and nothing to push away, with what can we be in conflict? When there is no possibility of losing or destroying anything, what can we grieve or fight? This text often uses the terms *bhava* and *abhava*, existence and nonexistence. These terms run through the most fundamental Buddhist teachings. In the four noble truths, the second truth is the cause of suffering, which is defined as craving for bhava and abhava. In the Buddhist doctrine of the twelvefold chain of dependent origination, craving leads to clinging, which leads to bhava, which is often translated as becoming. In simple terms, I want sunshine to exist when I don't see sunshine, so I suffer. I want the pain in my back not to exist, so I suffer.

The theme of the false duality of existence/nonexistence runs from the earliest layers of Buddhist teaching into later Mahayana and Vajrayana traditions. Yogacara teachings build on and uphold it, but they tend to focus on another duality: self and other, also known as cognizer and cognized, or seer and seen. This is a more distinctly Yogacara emphasis. What appears in each moment of experience is this false imagination of a self, which Yogacarins call *manas*, and a separate, observed world. The self and the other don't really exist as separate from each other, and the very nonduality of that relationship is essential, dharmata, reality, the teaching.

Tibetan visualization practices uphold the wisdom of this verse. They harness the power of imagination to dissolve dualities. One of the most common of these practices is visualizing a buddha. With eyes closed, we develop the ability to see—to have a visual experience of—a buddha. We can develop the ability to have increasingly vivid sensory experiences through imagination. For example, an average nonmusician may occasionally hear a brief little nagging tune in their mind, but through practice some composers can hear entire new orchestral musical pieces before they write them down. Practice is powerful! So we can form the image of the Buddha in the mind and develop the ability to see it in vivid detail. Then we practice seeing it as transparent, empty, and unreal. Finally we allow the image and ourselves to melt into one another. Deity visualization allows us to engage the imagination and then use it to help us dissolve the sense that we are separate from what we perceive, separate from Buddha, or that any of it is ultimately real.

This teaching does not deny the value of a shared sense of truth and facts. People believe things are facts based on their mental conditioning. What we call "facts" matter because they guide our actions. I have found myself in arguments where two people couldn't agree about the words someone had said five minutes earlier. In the United States today, millions of people are utterly convinced that there has been massive voter fraud, while other millions find this contention bizarre and baseless. I wasn't present at all the polling places. However, I believe that there wasn't massive voter fraud, because I trust the mainstream media and election officials on this particular point. Presenting folks convinced of voter fraud with the facts, I believe, rarely changes their opinion. Facts matter, but we arrive at what we call *facts* through collective mental processes. Our liberation and our bondage are dependent on these processes. The facts we share come from our shared sense of trust; damage to that fabric of trust has brought us to what some are now calling the "post-truth" era.

Yogacara practice is meant to help us and our communities see the world in a way that is beneficial, to find a collective understanding of the world that can help us heal. We need journalists and scientists because they can help us understand the world together, not because they deal in absolute truths, or are always right, but because they are a part of a shared process of investigation. Vasubandhu spent his life writing, engaging in dualistic thought, and also seeing beyond it. He created contexts where people of widely differing views across the landscape of Indian thought could move toward a sense of truth together. He wrote a seminal treatise on valid reasoning among folks of differing worldviews, and his student Dignaga, who carried his work forward, is now known as one of the architects of Indian theories of valid knowledge. They paved the way for a diverse culture to have a common ground for talking about what is true.

Buddhist teachings celebrate the importance of discernment about the relative or conventional truth of things, which Yogacarins call the imaginary nature. The Dalai Lama models this tradition, teaching that all things are empty of separate lasting nature and duality while also supporting inquiry with scientists, religious leaders, and politicians from around the world.

5

Mind Only

What is the unreal imagination there?
Mind. Since it is imagined like this,
Both how it is imagined and the thing imagined
Are ultimately thus, undiscoverable. ||5||

I feel my feet. The right one is resting on rough wooden slats, the left one is resting on the right. Knowing the body is at the heart of my practice. In Buddhist teaching the first foundation of mindfulness is mindfulness of body, and in Soto Zen we emphasize doing things with our whole selves. Our core practice, zazen, is sometimes simply called "posture and breath." I try to write with my whole body as a singer might sing from theirs. I recommend making this central to your practice: to allow, deepen, and return to awareness of the body.

These sensations in the feet are a part of what appears. Returning to the previous verse, they are false imagination since they appear as dual. It seems clear to me that I—a self—am aware of sensations in the feet, that the feet exist, and do not not-exist, and that they are not the floor. I don't have to write all this down or think about it to "know" it. These dualities appear directly in the experience of the moment. Here Vasubandhu shows that the false dualistic imagination that appears here is mind. My feet are mind!

It may be helpful to think of the word *mind* here as meaning "experience" or "awareness." Yogacara teachings, and to a lesser degree Buddhist teaching in general, emphasize things *as experienced*, not as absolutely real objects. For example, mindfulness of body is being aware of the experience of the body. This is different from a contemporary Western view of how to be aware of the body: to know how much it weighs, to know which regions of the brain correspond to which feelings, and to know how fast one can make it run three miles. Yogacara teachings say that dualism, the seeing of things as objects, is one of the central drivers of suffering. Feminist theory helps us see that objectifying the female body is harmful. Yogacara points out that this harmful tendency to objectify pervades our entire experience. But it's just a habit. Mindfulness of body is to know the body intimately, as sensation. It allows us to get a little closer to feeling the body, but not as an object. However, this is just a step on the path. With all my training in mindfulness of body, it often seems like I (a self) am observing feet sensations (an other), and that the feet exist and don't not-exist, and that the floor is not my feet. These dualities continue to appear, and these false imaginations are mind. Ultimately, we are invited here to leave objectification behind, to realize that mind and body are intimate and inseparable, nondual.

It is mind that makes these things appear as dual. It is mind that imagines them thus. We translate the Sanskrit term *citta* as "mind." *Citta* refers to mind in the broadest possible terms, as consciousness or awareness, and is sometimes translated as "thought." *Citta* also has a technical meaning in Buddhist Abhidharma, of which Vasubandhu was a renowned master, having written arguably the most revered text on this branch of Buddhist thought, the *Abhidharmakosa*. A *dharma* is an experiential moment: a shape, color, emotion, word, meaning, physical sensation, or smell. A citta, then, is a mental dharma: consciousness of sight, consciousness of body, consciousness of volition, sadness, hope, and so on.

There are hundreds of thousands of dharmas in your field of experience right now. If you engage your senses—sight, hearing, smell, taste, touch, and mind— you can notice thousands of colors, shapes, feelings, or sounds. Look around, feel, listen! Each one of these is either a citta (mind) dharma or depends on a citta dharma; every phenomena (dharma) in your field of experience appears to you only if there is awareness of the phenomena (citta dharma). For example, we see color only if we are aware of color. Vasubandhu is saying that each of these individual dharmas and the aggregated sense of them as a whole are what appears. What appears is false imagination, because it is dependent on citta, mind. None of it is ultimately real, because it is mind. The entirety of this moment depends on consciousness.

Consider the images in your left peripheral vision. You are probably aware of images, and you might have a sense that these images are of things separate from you. As you focus on them, your experience of them differs from before I called your attention there. There is no experiential moment, dharma, of a visual image separate from and not mediated by your awareness.

The first line of Vasubandhu's "Thirty Verses on Consciousness Only" states:

> Everything conceived as self or other occurs in the transformation of consciousness.

In the fifth verse of the text, he says:

> Both how it is imagined and the thing imagined are ultimately thus, undiscoverable.

The self which imagines, the process by which self and things are imagined, and the thing imagined are all just part of the mind or consciousness; they can't really be found. Can you find your mind? Where is it located? Can you find your feet? I suspect you can find awareness of your feet, but can you find your feet outside of your experience of them? Can you find the process by which you seem to experience them? Can you find exactly how the sensations in the feet are something other than the sensations of the floor with which they are in contact? We find these sorts of questions throughout Zen *koan* literature, the meditation methods of the *Surangama Sutra*, and in some Tibetan traditions.

If we really look, we will see that every aspect of our experience is characterized by a massive array of dualities, products of mind. They are found only in relation to mind. We are imagining our world.

In Yogacara, there are many ways of saying this, for example: *cittamatra,* mind-only, *vijnanamatra,* consciousness-only, and *vijnaptimatra,* projection-only. The main implications of this are twofold. First, when you are experiencing afflictive emotion, you can remember that the entirety of the situation is mind-only, false imagination, and you can wake up from the agony of the dream. Second, because everything we experience is imagination, the *way* you imagine is of utmost value and importance. You always have power and agency in how you engage and imagine right now. Everything you do always matters. The first verses of the *Dhammapada* state

Our life is shaped by our mind; we become what
    we think. Suffering follows an evil thought as the
    wheels of a cart follow the oxen that draws it.
Our life is shaped by our mind; we become what
    we think. Joy follows a pure thought like a
    shadow that never leaves.[8]

In Yogacara texts, thinking doesn't simply refer to
the stream of words that runs through our minds.
Instead, thinking refers to the totality of how we perceive the world, for all our perceptions are dependent
on cittas—they are mind. We know things only
through our way of experiencing. And remember, it is
our lives that are shaped by what *we* think. Suffering
and joy are collective, and in each thought, each sound,
each time we set a foot on the ground, we have an
opportunity to contribute something to the possibility
of collective liberation and healing.

6

Eight Consciousnesses

Mind is said to be twofold,
Cause and result,
Also called store consciousness and
Arising consciousness, which is sevenfold. ||6||

Karma is often defined as cause and effect. In Buddhism, karma is a way of explaining how and why our actions matter. Vasubandhu teaches that imagination is mind, and mind is twofold, having cause and effect. Mind, or imaginary nature, is anything that appears as dual, such as self and other or light and dark. In previous verses Vasubandhu told us dualities are not real, and now he introduces another duality: cause and result. Again and again, Vasubandhu will show that his words are not the ultimate truth, yet he keeps using them because they still matter. This verse is about why they matter.

The influential Mahayana teaching of the two truths states that there is relative or conventional truth—which roughly corresponds to the imaginary nature—and absolute truth or emptiness—which roughly corresponds to the complete, realized nature. In this verse we see most explicitly why Yogacara teachings use terms like imaginary, imputational, and mind-only. It is to create a framework for understanding why and how we can do things that lead to nonsuffering if everything is empty of self-nature. Cause and effect, also known as karma, is mental.

In this verse Vasubandhu introduces the eight consciousnesses. The eight-consciousness model and the model of the three natures are the two most influential teachings of Yogacara. The cause is the storehouse consciousness (*alaya vijnana*); the sevenfold result is every aspect of what we call experience: sights, sounds, smells, tastes, physical sensations, objects of mind, and the sense of being a self (manas).

The alaya vijnana, storehouse consciousness, is sometimes called store consciousness, root consciousness, or eighth consciousness. It is a way to describe the process of karma: mental, emotional, perceptual, and behavioral conditioning that creates our experience. It is an unconscious aspect of mind, so we don't experience it directly; my teacher Tim Burkett calls it the storehouse *un*conscious. It is variously described as a process, or a momentary phenomenon, like a river flowing, or a waterfall. Yogacara texts repeatedly remind us that the alaya is not lasting, fixed, or separate. It is the ever-changing ground in which the seeds of our actions—mental, physical, perceptual, and emotional—are planted. It is where they lie dormant and bear fruit. We will dig more deeply into this ground in the next few chapters. The key point here is that mind, the illusion in which we live, is where we have power. It is what causes results to occur.

The result aspect of mind is what appears in any given moment. Conditions—seeds in the storehouse—bear fruit, and there is a result. This result is sevenfold: manas, mind objects, sight, sound, smell, taste, and touch. Manas is sometimes called the consciousness of a self or the seventh consciousness. Pali Canon texts refer to a similar aspect of experience they call "I-making," "mine-making," and the conceit "I am." Manas is the sense that there is an "I," a subject, observing objects. Do you notice this aspect of your experience right now? Perhaps it seems like you are looking out at the world from behind your eyes. This sense is manas. Manas and alaya are both innovations of Yogacara, while the other six senses have been basic to Buddhist thought since the earliest teachings.

The remaining six types of consciousness are mind consciousness, *manovijnana*, and what in the West are considered the five senses. In this particular context, mind consciousness refers to the aspects of experience we usually consider mental, such as emotions and thoughts. In Buddhist psychology these six are all considered senses. They are things we can be aware of right now: anger, words, ineffable intuitions, a memory of the smell of garlic in oil, a child's soft palm resting in your own, the radiance of the sun on the horizon, thoughts, a pain in the neck, the roar of a distant motorcycle, bliss, despair, cool breeze on the skin, fear, cloth against the belly as we inhale . . . They're all just something that appears. The Buddha called these six senses "the All."

Vasubandhu says mind is cause, or alaya (the unknowable process of conditioning that produces our experience), and result, or manas (a sense of being a self observing things), along with all of the things we observe. In the third verse of his "Thirty Verses" he acknowledges that there may be absolutely real distinct things, but he states that they can't ultimately be known, because we know things only through the process of our consciousness.

For many of us this is a difficult claim to take seriously. I was raised to believe that matter, energy, desks, atoms, and such are absolutely real. Our lives emerge from this absolutely real matter. This teaching reminds us that we don't experience anything outside of the field of our conditioned, habitual way of looking at things. Taking up this view can have a real and valuable impact.

Heidi Larson is a medical anthropologist who is currently focused on vaccination. She is internationally known for her effectiveness in promoting public health. The scientific consensus on the safety and effectiveness of vaccines is extensive, and yet millions of people choose to not use them. Their reasons are many. I have seen countless bitter exchanges between people who choose not to use vaccines and people who do. Larson believes vaccines save lives but are effective only if people will take them. She spends her time trying to understand people's opinions, feelings, and ideas about vaccines so she can take action that will promote our welfare. She wrote that she is "inspired by a feeling that the conversation between the scientific/medical community and the public was 'stuck' between the scientists and health professionals inhibited about going into what feels to them to be messy, emotional, unscientific discussions, while publics . . . feel that scientists and medical professionals are elite, emotionless, and unwilling to listen to their genuine concerns, questions, and feeling." She focuses on understanding that we are all motivated by conditioned views, rather than on explaining things she believes are absolutely true or forcing people to do things. The power of her work is based in creating contexts for listening, understanding, dialogue, and trust.[9]

7

Seeds and Fruit

First it is called mind (*citta*) because
It is full of (*citatvāt*) seeds of afflictive tendencies.
Second it is called mind (*citta*) because
It is the arising of various (*citra*) appearances. ||7||

The storehouse, alaya, is full of karmic seeds, and the result is the amazing variety of things we experience. Here Vasubandhu makes a play on words. He says that the word *citta* as it applies to the storehouse is related to the word *citatvāt*, which means "full of," because it's full of karmic seeds. The world *citta,* as it applies to the manas and the six senses, is related to the word *citra* which means "various," because it has so much variety. The distant accordion I hear right now, the hammering sounds of construction, the ache in my eyes as I face the sun, the feelings you are experiencing in this moment, people's diverse responses to a news story—such a variety of things appear! The puns in this verse bear a striking resemblance to those in a Pali Canon sutra where the Buddha teaches that all suffering and wellness depend on mind. He speaks of a painted picture (citra) of the various (also citra) realms that beings experience dependent on karma, and how this picture depends on the variety of minds (citta).[10] Using word-play, Buddha blurs the lines between what is painted, minds, and lived experiences in all their diversity.

It is so sad to see just how full the mind is of afflictive tendencies. We find ourselves dully scrolling on a screen, or inexplicably bereft while walking down a rainy street, or annoyed with ourselves or our colleagues. We see people tear their lives apart for the pleasure or numbness of drugs and alcohol, and we see them falling into the same tortured relationships. When we turn on the news, we learn that people are killed, or that they steal, and deny that harm is being done while railing against others. Together we tear at the subtle fabric of interdependence that supports billions of living beings as we chase temporary safety, pleasure, or convenience. Samsara, the wheel of suffering, rolls on, powerful and vast. From a Buddhist perspective all of this is produced by mind. Yogacara gives us the metaphor of karmic seeds in the field of mind to help us see that we can cultivate wellness.

James Baldwin once wrote, "People pay for what they do, and still more for what they have allowed themselves to become. And they pay for it simply; by the lives they lead." A central tenet of Buddhist thought is that each action produces a similar result. If you feel angry and shout, you plant seeds of anger and shouting in the storehouse. If you feel calm and confident and ask someone to stop doing something harmful, you plant seeds in the storehouse of calm and assertiveness. If you open an online shopping site each time you feel sad, you plant seeds of sadness, avoidance, and consumption. Those seeds will bear fruit, though we don't know when or where. Our tendencies toward feelings and actions in any moment are the result of conditioning that goes back farther than any of us can comprehend. As the Buddha says many times in the Pali Canon, these tendencies are "without discoverable beginning." Traumas, joys, insights, and countless moments of calm going back generations bring us this moment. The impulse to recoil from the discomfort that you experience when sweat drips into your eyes on a hot day couldn't have appeared without microorganisms recoiling from stimuli millions of years ago.

But here is the good news and the central thesis of Buddhism: you are not merely a victim of karma. You always have the capacity to do something beneficial. In each moment you can respond to what is arising (the results of karma) with something that will plant karmic seeds for future benefit. Karma is the way to understand why what you do matters, and how you can do something that will promote true well-being. The Buddhist idea of karma is fundamentally about empowerment.

In the Pali Canon, Buddha teaches that karma is intention (*cetana*). Here intention means the things, both conscious and subconscious, that cause you to act. Your thoughts, the ways you view your environment, your emotions, your bodily sensations—these are your karma. Whether you are contributing to suffering or to well-being is determined by them. In any second there are millions of karmic seeds bearing fruit and appearing as cittas in a various display! Think of how many concepts the mind must apply to make just this moment of experience appear to you as it does. You are unconsciously identifying dozens of colors and count-less shapes, distinguishing one sense from another, trying to follow my meaning, and experiencing a vari-ety of sensations in the body, most of them ignored. We experience emotions so subtle we can barely detect or name them.

Amid this torrential flow, the central question I ask is, "What can I offer that is beneficial?" From a Yoga-cara perspective there are some consistent answers: mindfulness of body and emotions, cultivation of awareness of interdependence and nonduality, and actions of body, speech, and mind that emerge from those four root practices.

I will emphasize mindfulness of emotions for now. This practice is the most powerful tool we have to diminish afflictive emotions. Practically speaking, mindfulness of body is entwined with mindfulness of emotions. Being aware of a racing heart, tension in the neck, or relaxation in the belly deepens awareness of emotion. When we experience afflictive emotions such as anger, despair, anxiety, or desire we are experiencing the fruit of previous karma. However, within each moment of awareness we can plant new seeds. By being mindful of our emotions, we plant seeds of compassion. Previous emotional conditioning is exhausted in the light of mindfulness, which is simply compassionate awareness. A simple formula for understanding this comes from the Pali Canon. The Buddha taught that karma is intention, which in this case means everything that consciously and subconsciously motivates your behavior. In the Anguttara Nikaya, Buddha says, "actions [karmas] willed, performed, and accumulated will not become extinct as long as their results have not been experienced."[11] When you experience a difficult emotion, you are experiencing the fruit of conditioning; by directly experiencing the emotion, you can allow it to become extinct. We generally don't do this when a difficult emotion arises. Rather than being mindful of the emotion itself, we become entranced by the mental activity that co-arises with the emotion. Rather than mindful experiencing of the feeling of anxiety, we obsess about a problem at work or with a family member. Rather than deeply knowing what anger feels like, we think about how horrible someone else is. Thus we ignore our feelings and plant the seeds for similar obsessions in the future.

As Audre Lorde wrote in her essay "Poetry Is Not a Luxury," "The quality of light by which we scrutinize our lives has a direct bearing upon the product which we live, and upon the changes which we hope to bring about through those lives." She saw the power of deeply knowing how we feel. Compassionate awareness of our emotions and intentions transforms our lives and the world around us. It is important to note that sometimes we don't have the inner resources to bear deep witness to our suffering, so it's good to find support and practices that can help us care for our own well-being.

As we focus on the idea of mind as the cause and result of experience, it's important to remember that this doesn't mean it's all about you. The sense that there is a "you" separate from other things (manas), is merely one of the various illusory appearances that result from karma. This does not mean that nothing matters—in fact, just the opposite. What you do always matters, even if, and precisely because you are unaware of it. Ignorance—ignoring—is one of the three principal categories of karma: desire, aversion, and delusion/ignorance. Mindfulness is important because it allows you to see the things happening that you usually ignore, things that will produce future experience. Learning that some of your jokes make people feel bad opens the door to healing. Dispelling ignorance about the impact of beef consumption on cows and on the ecology of the planet has karmic impact. What is the price of feeling so separate from our animal kin? In the United States people are often unaware of our overseas drone campaigns and constant warfare, or the terrible conditions of our domestic criminal justice system, all of which we pay for with our taxes. The harm these systems inflict depends on our ignorance of the totality of our interdependence. Facing our ignorance can be painful, but ultimately it is less painful than the alienation that comes from turning away.

To be clear, the teaching that life is shaped by mind doesn't mean that when we imagine getting a new shiny car, we will necessarily get a new shiny car. Imagining getting a new shiny car plants seeds of desire, among other things. It creates the conditions for believing that some material object we don't have will make us happy. It bears fruit in a life of waiting for satisfaction.

An important theme of many teachings on karma is that we don't know when the seeds we plant will bear fruit. When you feel a pang of irritation, that could be the fruit of irritation from thousands of years before, last week, or two seconds ago. A vast array of karmic seeds are latent in the storehouse. I know people who have been through years of therapy, read countless wellness books, practiced meditation, and attended retreats, yet they still suffer a great deal. People have given their lives, literally, to nonviolent movements for liberation. Hundreds of us spent months occupying the street outside the fourth police precinct in Minneapolis after a police officer killed Jamar Clark, yet the next year an officer killed Philando Castile, and in 2020 another officer murdered George Floyd. Although the violence goes on, every day people gather at George Floyd Square, to heal and to envision real public safety. Where there is rage or despair let us offer compassion, and let us not give up.

Yogacara teachings uphold the third paramita, *ksanti*, endurance. Ksanti is to trust that our practice matters, and to keep going even if it appears that it does not. Classic teachings on ksanti focus on cultivating love and nonviolence in the face of suffering. They are about never forgetting our true power. Social scientists are demonstrating the power and effectiveness of nonviolent social movements, and we are seeing the science on the benefits of meditation pile up. Ultimately, the impact of putting love and care into the world is beyond measure. Karma is without discoverable beginning, and the seeds we plant bear fruit, we know not when. Angela Davis once said, "Sometimes we have to do the work even though we don't yet see a glimmer on the horizon that it's actually going to be possible." Along with ksanti, Buddhist teachings encourage us to cultivate *mudita*, altruistic joy. Or, as Cornel West once said, "The only way to be a long-distance freedom fighter is to find joy in the struggle. Joy in empowering others." As we walk the path of liberation, I hope you will plant seeds of joy along the way. Take time to simply see a cloud in the sky, to gaze up into the limbs of a tree or down into a spider's glistening web, to hold a friend in your arms, to laugh at our foibles, to listen to the babbling of a passing child, and keep going.

8

A Threefold Illusion

In brief, the unreal imagination
Is considered threefold.
Ripening, thus caused,
Or else appearance. ||8||

This verse parallels the opening of Vasubandhu's "Thirty Verses":

> Everything conceived as self or other occurs in the transformation of consciousness.
>
> This transformation has three aspects:
> The ripening of karma, the consciousness of a self, and the imagery of sense objects.[12]

The totality of experience is something we are always imagining, conceiving, and creating. To focus on our capacity to heal and create freedom from suffering, it is beneficial to view this whole process as having three aspects: alaya, manas, and the six senses. This is simply another way of remembering and thinking about the eight consciousnesses. This verse subtly emphasizes how all these aspects appear to arise, to change, and pass away. Embedded in the compound translated here as "unreal imagination" is the term *bhuta*, which refers to something that has come into being. Fundamental to our imagination of the world is that it seems to be made of things that come to be.

I hear the sound of a plane come into being in the distance, and I feel this distinct breath in my belly arise. I touch the heater by my side to test whether it is working. I feel heat coming into being. I am here feeling these things, yet I, someday, will pass away. Vasubandhu keeps reminding me to think of these phenomena as imaginations, and that anything coming into being at any time is an imagination. None of it exists without conceiving.

Frida Kahlo painted many self-portraits that depicted her growing from and bound to vegetal roots and the ground. She was deeply curious about the self and transformation, as well as how we are bound to the past and to the Earth. We see all these themes reflected in Vasubandhu's verse. Kahlo once wrote, "*Nada es absoluto. Todo cambia, todo se mueve, todo gira, todo vuela y desaparece.*" Or, "Nothing is absolute. Everything changes, everything moves, everything revolves, everything flies and disappears."

In Buddhist thought, coming into being is always inextricably tied to passing away, to impermanence. As Soto Zen founder Dogen once said, "When you practice intimately and return to where you are, it will be clear that nothing at all has unchanging self."[13] In the *Satipatthana Sutta*, we are instructed to watch particular aspects of experience arise and pass away. Buddhist teachings in general invite us to deeply see impermanence so that we may realize the futility of trying to base our security on things that we will surely lose: the self, our loved ones, sensual pleasures, or achievements. They promise that we can find a deep embodied trust that is not dependent on ideas or things, a state of bliss and compassionate action that is unconditional.

One winter, I spent a couple weeks in solo retreat in the snowy bluffs of Hokyoji in southern Minnesota. Each time I walked into the small meditation room, I passed a calligraphy with four-foot-tall Chinese characters that meant "no birth, no death." This classic Zen phrase is sometimes translated, "no arising, no ceasing," or "no coming, no going." The message of this verse is that things coming into being are only imagination.

It is a habit to think that because we experience time as linear—as a series of things coming to be and passing away—linear time is real. The growing cultural awareness of the impact of trauma is starting to soften conventional views on sharp divisions of time and identity. It is well-documented that shame and corporal punishment will change a child's behavior in the short term. It can make them sit down and shut up. It is also well-documented that children who are disciplined with shame and corporal punishment are much more likely to experience poverty, addiction, behavioral problems, and incarceration. It appears that the phenomenon of a cowed child told to sit down and shut up arose at one time, while the phenomenon of an officer pushing someone into the back of a police car arose at another, but these are in fact interdependent. The illusion of momentary control is always dependent on ignoring vast unknowable impacts.

With analytical meditation we come to understand that we can't locate borders between the present moment, the past, and the future. With video editing tools you might say that you can find the precise moment an image appears, but actually no editing tools exist with infinitely small divisions of time. And besides, the image you perceive is always constructed over a span of time through billions of neural activities in the brain.

Albert Einstein once said, "Time and space are modes by which we think, and not conditions in which we live." To be honest, I don't understand physics well enough to know why he would say this, but my Buddhist practice helps me see why it is beneficial to understand the arising of things as imaginary. Knowing that habitually perceiving things a certain way does not make them absolutely true helps me stay humble. Humility is a doorway to freedom from the confines of certainty. Certainty requires ignoring, being unaware of, or denying possibilities beyond my way of looking at things. In Buddhist karmic terms, certainty is the fruit and the seed of delusion. Of course, we sometimes need a sense of certainty to have emotional stability. When I am with someone who feels ethically or emotionally ungrounded, I encourage them to find a connection to their bodily sensations, to what they see and hear, to their feelings, to their healthiest relationships, and to their deepest values. It may not be the time for them to focus on cutting through certainty. It may, though, be the moment we see through time.

About twenty-five years ago, I was sitting in a circle of men on hard-backed chairs in a small room with a single window facing a pale gray sky. On the wall beside me was one poster with the Twelve Steps and another that said, "Learn to name your feelings: angry, sad, happy, excited, afraid, ashamed, anxious, calm . . ." My body ached and trembled. I was nauseated, but I felt far better than the day before. I knew exactly where the nearest bar was. The inside of my mouth was begging for liquor. A young man with a cast was waiting to see if he would ever recover the use of an arm he had crushed during an overdose. An old man with a pancreas destroyed by alcohol talked vaguely of plans for after his release from the facility. I shared my story, and I listened to the stories in the circle. My attention settled on the voices of these men, struggling to be honest, to be real with one another, to stay sober for one more day. I felt the vastness of the suffering, and something else hard to describe. I sensed that the possibility of wellness, the caginess and the caring, the hard chair against my thighs and the gray square of pale sky, the hope, the despair, the harm, the anguish, the joy, and all the stories in that room were not a matter of now and then, or now and some imagined future. Together in our brokenness, we were whole in the circle of all times.

9

Cause and Effect

The first is the root consciousness
For it is characterized by ripening.
The others are the arising consciousnesses;
They are the active cognition of seer and seen. ||9||

Verse 8 says that mind is one thing, imaginary, and it
should be considered threefold. In Verses 6 and 9 Vasubandhu describes it as twofold. There are many ways to
look at things! Can we take this teaching to heart? As he
works to keep us holding these ideas lightly, and binds
them together in this verse, Vasubandhu emphasizes
two themes in relation to the eight consciousnesses of
our experience: Cause and result are imagination, and
perceiving is an activity.

Recall that the cause is alaya, the storehouse, and the
result is manas, objects of mind (such as thoughts and
emotions), as well as sights, sounds, scents, flavors, and
feeling. Our experience ripens from the karma in our
store consciousness. However in the previous verse,

ripening is included in what he calls "this imagination," and when Vasubandhu first introduces the primacy of mind, citta, he calls it "false imagination." All elements of the eight consciousness are included in the illusory category, which includes both cause and effect. How can something illusory cause things to happen?

In Vasubandhu's "Twenty Verses on Consciousness Only" he addresses the question of how something imaginary can cause real results. He makes a surprising analogy; an erotic dream can produce semen in the physical world. There is so much evidence that what we imagine impacts reality. Imagine walking down a darkened street alone and seeing a large, male figure fast approaching down an alley with a bat in his hand. How would your body react? As he nears you realize it's a dear friend saying, "Hi! I'm just heading home from softball practice."

Imagination matters. When we spend the day thinking up horrible outcomes for a meeting, it affects how we act. You can imagine creating an organization to heal community wounds, and lo and behold, the organization may come to be. When I imagine a car accident I was in years ago, I feel my pulse increase, my body tense. Visualization is widely used in sports training because science shows it works to improve players' performance. Studies show that visualizing making free throws can be almost as effective as practicing making free throws.[14]

However, all the "real" physical data I cited above is also imaginary according to the three natures; we know it only as we experience it. The *Lankavatara Sutra* states:

But karma isn't real
thus to make their minds let go
of what grasps and what is grasped
I liken it to waves.
Their body, possessions, and the world
This is what they're conscious of
This is how their karma appears
Just like surging waves.[15]

Karma is the cause of the appearance of body, possessions, the world, and the totality of what we're conscious of, including what grasps, the sense of a self experiencing things, and what is grasped—all the things. Karma is like waves, sometimes terrifying, sometimes beautiful. Sometimes we drift and wish it would never end, and sometimes we're near drowning. It seems so real. It's not just that what we experience is illusory. What this body of teaching says causes experience, the alaya, is *also* not real. It can't be because this teaching is of an imaginary nature, too. We are imagining it right now! Karma isn't real, it's just a word, a way of looking at things, to help us to be free of grasping.

To return to my earlier question: How can some-thing illusory cause something to happen? In a way it can't. The great Yogacara philosopher Dharmakirti wrote, "Only an entity capable of producing an effect is ultimately existent."[16] The longer answer Vasu-bandhu offers is that an illusory thing can't really *cause* something to happen, it only *seems* like it does, and that this matters because we live in a world of seeming. Our lived reality is an imagination. Believing that what we experience is the ripening of karma in our storehouse, and it can help us imagine something better, help us to let go of our anguish, anxiety, selfishness, and alien-ation, and embody our liberative, healing power.

In the Pali Canon the Buddha teaches that after his awakening he is no longer subject to karma, yet he still devotes his life to simple living, meditation, and serv-ing his community. From a Yogacara perspective, his awakening was realizing that he wasn't bound by karma. His awakening was truly understanding the imaginary nature, and he continued to devote himself to this understanding by meeting each person where they were with his best idea for what would help them be free.

A common argument against the idea that cause and effect is imaginary goes something like this: If gravity doesn't have real effects, try jumping out of a fifth-floor window. My understanding is that folks chose not to jump off cliffs and that birds deftly sailed the winds for thousands of years before Isaac Newton theorized gravity in the seventeenth century. Yogacara teachings claim, and there appear to be, vast commonalities, dependent on conditions, in how beings view the world. When people began to accept Newton's theory of gravity it had profound effects, as did the adoption of Einstein's different theory of gravity. Their science impacts our experience. Yogacara encourages us to consider, though, that what is most important is the intentional qualities that we bring to science. Greed, fear, hatred and ignoring interdependence have brought us to an ecological crisis and have brought us arsenals that could destroy almost all planetary life at the push of a button. People also bring compassion and awareness of interdependence and impermanence into the sciences. Think of the pioneering work of Jane Goodall, who has immersed herself in the lives of chimpanzees, as well as that of countless ecologists and doctors who do not fight death, but face life and death together in their work.

I embrace the understanding of cause and effect that I suspect many of my readers share: Cause and effect is a property of physical objects and energy. When I give my son a hug, it has an effect on his body. When I buy a phone, my choice has an effect on countless lives who worked to produce that phone, as well as on soil, plants, and insects. This view of matter as primary is called materialism. However, my Yogacara practice has also brought me to embrace the understanding that this materialist view is just a way of looking at things produced by consciousness—my habits of mind, my karma. I embrace both of these views because I have some trust that they are beneficial.

Before I made a radical commitment to sobriety, I was certain of the sources of all the chaos of my life: my own worthlessness, the vindictiveness of the cops, the drama of the people around me, the pointless conventions of society. Somehow the problem never seemed to be intoxication. To my mind it was the only reasonable solution. When I was learning how not to drink and use drugs, which had almost cost me my life, I came to believe that alcohol, cocaine, marijuana, and pills entering my body caused things to spiral out of control. The cause and result of using them were painfully evident. The materialist understanding that drugs were the problem helped me survive and to manifest what has become a joyful life that I couldn't have even imagined in the early days of recovery. Ultimately, though, my recovery from addiction wasn't about not using drugs, it was about transforming my consciousness. It is this transformation which causes—and is—freedom from addiction. The way I see things changes. Buddhist teachings allow us to shift our attention to see more clearly what causes suffering and what we can do to heal. This brings me to the second theme of this verse: Perceiving is an activity.

We don't passively receive the reality of the world through our senses and then respond to it. The world we experience is created; it is "the active cognition of seer and seen." Our life is created by our karma, and we create karma in every moment. We have the power to plant seeds that will create a better world. This body of teachings emphasizes the impact of each moment of intentionality. Our power lies in the quality of heart and mind we offer to the moment. Why do I think this worldview is more effective than materialism for healing our suffering and freeing us from collective modes of violence, oppression, and destruction? I will answer with some lines from a Chinese Chan nun named Baochi who wrote:

> The vastness of karmic consciousness is hard to prove
> But when Mr. Zhang drinks, then Mr. Li gets drunk.[17]

Sometimes I get a call or I see an obituary telling me that another friend of mine has died from addiction. I've lost a dozen friends so far, and I can never know what part my enabling of their intoxication played or the impact their deaths and addictions will have on future generations of their families. The web is too complex to map with materialist tools. I can never know the impact of the thousands of hours I've spent working with addicts in recovery, either. I have witnessed the awakening of so much freedom!

One of Baochi's inspirations, the great Chan nun Miaozong, wrote:

> When outside the diamond door he glowered
> Inside the stable the wooden horse's face turned
>   red.[18]

In the verse above, there is no physical connection between the man's glower and the wooden horse's face, and yet there is reaction and connection. We cannot ultimately know when or where the results of any karmic seed will manifest—but manifest they will. Miaozong wrote her lines in a Chan compilation she created in the twelfth century, but could she have known that in the seventeenth century Baochi and her Dharma sister, Zukui, looking to revive the rarely recorded teachings of a female master of Chan, would pull them from obscurity and write their own commentaries, or that Beata Grant in the twenty-first would again revive them in English?

I believe that buying a chunk of an animal killed thousands of miles away, or offering a caring smile for a person on the street, as well as each tiny moment of anxiety, desire, or compassion you cultivate has an impact on every living being. I can't measure it. Miaozong says "the wooden horse's face turns red." A wooden horse is a classic Buddhist metaphor for something that has no reality or causal agency, like the horns of a rabbit, a wooden man, or a stone woman. Miaozong invites us into a worldview of mystery, where we don't know or see what is ultimately real, but where an angry glare causes suffering we can't calculate, where a smile has radiance beyond the limits of our knowing, where our actions really matter. All of this isn't real, but it's as real as it gets.

10

Free from Within Duality

Because affliction and cessation are both
Existent and nonexistent, both dual and one,
Not different in characteristics,
These natures are said to be profound. ||10||

"Freedom is thus, not being liberated from samsara, but not being afflicted in it." These are words from Vasubandhu's commentary on his half-brother Asanga's *Mahayanasamgraha* (*A Compendium of the Mahayana*), called *Mahayanasamgraha-bhasya*.[19] *Samsara*, the world of affliction, is the cycle of *dukkha* (suffering) we find ourselves in. We want to be done sweeping the floor or for the sun to come out, we wish we were thinner or that we had more hair. We have small nagging anxieties as well as burdens we collectively bear in our own distinct ways: trauma, despair, rage, hunger, death, illness, violence, shame, addiction, domination. Nirvana is the cessation of this suffering. It is the opposite of samsara. Vasubandhu upholds the central theme of Mahayana Buddhism: We are called to remain in samsara for the liberation of everyone. We are not called to escape in the Mahayana, but to remain, and remain free from affliction amid it all. Nirvana and samsara are one. We are not liberated from samsara, but we find liberation in samsara.

This verse marks a shift. The last several chapters have focused on the eight consciousnesses. Here Vasubandhu sets the table for the next eleven verses, all of which will deal with the relationship of the three natures to each other and to existence and nonexistence, duality and oneness, difference and nondifference, affliction and cessation. The three natures are distinct, and Vasubandhu has been defining and laying out their characteristics and differences. As he says here, they are also "not different in characteristics." Both views are valuable. The underpinning of this section is nonduality. Usually we experience the world in terms of dualities: I and everything else, my hand and things that aren't my hand, suffering and happiness, samsara and nirvana, good and evil. Nondualism suggests that none of these polarities are ultimately real; they are simply habituated ways of looking at things. However, nondualism doesn't claim that they are all one. Oneness and duality are a duality. This teaching says they too are nondual. It's helpful to train the mind to think about nonduality; we can also experience it. During a retreat, my teacher's Zen teacher, Shunryu Suzuki, told a story of visiting a Rinzai Zen teacher named Tanker. Tanker was very large and rather intimidating in style, and he challenged students in order to help them shatter their patterned ways. Suzuki was known for being very small in stature and embodying a joyful, unimposing manner of Zen living. After a few days in retreat, unclear about how to relate to this very different teacher, Suzuki walked into the interview room in a deep state of concentration and realized, as he put it, "I am Tanker." He didn't believe he had disappeared. The duality was gone, but nothing was destroyed or left out.

One of the most prevalent Buddhist teachings on nondualism is known as the two truths. This teaching is more widely known than the three natures. The two truths are associated with the Madhyamaka school. The two truths *samvriti* and *paramartha* are often translated as "relative" and "absolute," or "conventional" and "ultimate." In East Asian Buddhist traditions they are alluded to in less technical terms such as *form* and *emptiness*, *light* and *dark*, *guest* and *host*, *difference* and *sameness*. I'll provide a brief explanation to show the kinship between the two truths and the three natures.

Things arise dependent on conditions. This is a central idea in Buddhist thought, going back to the earliest teachings: "Because of this, that." You see your friend, so you feel happy, so you smile. This dependency is the pivot on which the two truths is constructed. In the example I just gave there is a smile. It is dependent on the friend, the happiness, and on an unbelievably vast number of conditions we didn't take the time to mention. This means it is empty, *sunya*. It is empty of any separate or lasting identity. It is merely the conventional way we describe or experience this mass of dependencies. Put another way, it exists only as relative to this web of things without which it is not. Each thing we name or experience as distinct is subject to this analysis. Insofar as they exist they are conventional, relative. This is known as conventional or relative truth. However, they are still characterized by emptiness, *sunyata*, devoid of separate or lasting identity. This emptiness is understood as absolute or ultimate truth. There is not a thing to which one can have attachment. Using dependency as the reason, the two truths proves that things are both relative and empty of this relative nature. That there is a smile is a relative, conventional truth. That the smile is empty, devoid of independent existence, is the ultimate truth. The truths are separate distinct truths because they are inseparable. They are nondual. The problem is that we usually see only the conventional truth. We get stuck on it and thus suffer and cause harm, but if we can also see the ultimate truth, we see the nirvana in samsara.

The three natures correspond closely to the two truths. The imaginary nature of things is how they appear to us as distinct, like the conventional truth. The complete, realized nature is that they are empty of dualities, like the ultimate truth. The dependent nature is that the "object" in question is dependent on conditions. The two truths essentially say that things have a relative truth and absolute truth *because they are dependent*. The three natures say they have imaginary nature, and complete, realized nature and *have the nature of being dependent*.

Over the past fifteen hundred years the two truths have been more widely taught than the three natures. As Buddhism came to East Asia, people there saw a commonality between the indigenous Taoist framework of yin/yang and the absolute and relative truth. Yin resembles the absolute: formless, undifferentiated, and mysterious. Yang is clear, distinct, and delineated like the relative. A twofold teaching meshed best with the Tao, and East Asian cultures were less attracted to the highly technical psychology of Abhidharma which constitutes Yogacara's imaginary nature. In Tibet, the two truths are favored because some Yogacara teachings suggest that mind is the fundamental basis for reality. This idea runs counter to key Buddhist teachings, so Tibetans generally consider the three natures a provisional, subsidiary teaching to the two truths. However, in verses five and thirty-six of our text, Vasubandhu explicitly states that mind is not an ultimately real thing.

Philosophically minded folks may find these points oversimplified, as there are mountains of very detailed philosophical disputations running back almost two thousand years on these subjects. However, to support our practice, this is a straightforward way of understanding. The two truths run throughout Mahayana thought to help us cut through our rigidity and delusions. The three natures offer a similar perspective but emphasize why our actions matter. By saying that what the two truths calls "relative" is imaginary, Yogacara teachings drive home a key point; we are active agents in creating the world we experience. Because they emphasize mental processes, the three natures are an excellent framework for understanding Buddhism for a culture that is interested in psychology. Also, by elevating dependency to a central, explicit place in the rubric, the three natures call us into awareness of interdependence. Awareness that everything is always collective is one of the most profound needs of our suffering world. Dr. King once wrote about why and how to dismantle poverty, racism, and militarism, saying, "All this is simply to say that all life is interrelated."

This may seem too heady, but much of Thich Nhat Hanh's genius for popularizing engaged Buddhism and mindfulness practice has been rooted in bringing the three natures to the masses. He emphasizes the eight consciousness teachings, or planting seeds and awareness of interdependence. He brings these teachings that cut through duality into day-to-day life. Like the best Zen teachers, he shows that nonduality can be embodied.

Tomoe Katagiri was my teacher in sewing the Buddhist robes that symbolize my ordination. Zen sewing is done as an expression of our practice and our vow to free all beings from suffering. Tomoe had a small, plain room with an altar where we would offer incense, bows, and chants before and after sewing. Generally, in a Soto Zen service we bow together, but the teacher leads. As the teacher leans forward the rest of the bodies follow. Tomoe was my teacher but was not ordained and sometimes seemed deferential as I was the one preparing for ordination. I wanted to show my respect and appreciation by really following how she took care of simple things, but there was something I just couldn't figure out. I asked, "Tomoe-san, during the service, are you leading the bows, or am I?" She looked me right in the eyes and said, "Yes."

11

Relax, This Really Matters

Both grasped as existing and really not existing,
The imaginary nature is considered
To have the characteristic
Of existence and nonexistence. ||11||

There's a classic Chinese story about a monkey precariously dangling from a tree branch over a pool of water and trying to reach down and scoop up the moon. She's grasping at a reflection and likely to be taking a cold unwanted swim. The moon is a common symbol for enlightenment. The foolish monkey strains to grasp something that cannot be held onto but is right before our eyes.

Dvayagraha, twofold grasping, is an important concept in Yogacara. Grasping here refers to what happens when a subject sees something as an object. The I, manas, arises from conditions in the storehouse and perceives everything else to be other: smells, raindrops, thunderclaps, the world. That primal duality drives the process of our suffering and is inherently bound to clinging. We may think we cling to money, but money is also holding us. At the climax of Vasubandhu's "Thirty Verses on Consciousness Only" he says, "when there is nothing to grasp, there is no grasping." We can let go of our tendency to cling to impermanent things, crave things we don't have, struggle for control, or hoard tools and weapons to defend ourselves. When there is no I, it does not make things, and there is no grasping. Manas ceases to function; Buddhist practice helps it to let go.

Things exist because we imagine that they do, and our belief in their existence is a kind of grasping. It is a fundamental driver of all our clinging. The imaginary nature doesn't exist, because the I—and all the other things it makes appear as separate things—are not real. They are just habits of mind. This is why it helps to relax: It helps us to slow down and see what's really here.

When I was a child, I was terrified that some horror was about to emerge from under the bed. It helped to look under it. Every night I struggled through the fear to make myself look. I never found any monsters! Finally, I could rest. What I thought existed had an enormous impact on me. We are all like this. We experience joy and suffering based on what we think exists.

Buddhism is not a life hack. If you read this verse and think, "No problem, since it's all imaginary, I'll just ignore it," you will just be caught in another web of your mind's creation. To truly let go is a matter of practice.

What you and I and everyone else thinks is real (the imaginary nature) is where we are living, so it matters to us. If we are interested in alleviating suffering, then we need to do it here. I feel grumpy when I see people in my neighborhood set up a table in the park and try to convince others that the Earth is flat. That is very real to me! It's likely that there are people whose views you find repugnant, ridiculous, and incomprehensible. Their viewpoint clearly matters to you. I am a Buddhist, so I believe everyone in every moment has the capacity to do things that are conducive to well-being, healing, and liberation. Each one of us has this capacity within our current frame of experience. Focusing on placing blame and viewing folks as alien or other isn't very helpful. Recognizing that we are all coming from our own perspective, and that this is the only place from which we can find some beneficial action, really helps. Like that little child in my bedroom years ago, we want someone who will get down on the floor and look under the bed with us so we can see that there are no monsters. We don't need someone to stand in the doorway and say, "Go to bed, it's all in your head."

The Tibetan text *The Ultimate Supreme Path of Mahamudra* states:

Those who ignore karma
and malign relative methods
are like birds without wings;
they will surely fall into the abyss of lower
    existences.
Therefore avoid even the smallest bad action,
and practice even the smallest good action.[20]

The imaginary nature, our experience, matters because we grasp it as existing: our worries about the job interview, our frustration with our spouses, our struggles with harmful eating habits, our failing health, the anguish of loss, our rage at gross injustice, or even petty slights. These are our lives! This is why it matters and why it really helps to relax. Take time to let your senses settle. We can plant seeds of thought, emotion, and action that create the conditions for a better future. Our lives matter too much for us to simply enact our habits. If we slow down, we have time to see what drives us and to become clear about what we truly want to offer to the world. It is the quality of intention that we offer in each moment that creates the world we imagine together.

Katagiri Roshi used to say, "Life is an emergency case." This moment is of the utmost importance. Katagiri was an inspiration to many dear and wonderful friends of mine because he met life fully with care, simplicity, humor, and a deep commitment to the stillness of meditation. He held it lightly. His response to the emergency of life was to slow down.

I came to Zen because I was overwhelmed with shame, despair, anxiety, and rage. I could not bear the angst that arose from my relationships. With practice I found that I could transform those relationships by giving up the illusion of control. I began to see that though I tried to control my circumstances, my grasping was binding me. Zen practice gave me an opportunity to do things without needing to get something or get away. I was invited into the mystery of noncontrol, the intimacy of each moment. I learned to sit with compassion in the fires of my own heart, take care of simple tasks wholeheartedly, embody the slow and focused bows of Soto Zen, immerse myself in stillness, sit face-to-face with my teacher, pick up a broom, and let go.

12

Painting the Moon in Water

Since it exists as an illusion, and does not exist
As it appears, the dependent
Is considered to have the characteristic
Of existence and nonexistence. ||12||

Let's return to the story of the monkey grasping at the moon in the water. So foolish! Early in the twentieth century, Fukuda Kodojin created a scroll painting called "Monkey Playing with the Moon Reflected on the Water." A smiling monkey dangling over a pool trails his fingers around the circle of the moon's reflection. The figure the monkey traces is also an *enso*, the open circle that is a classic image of Zen. Kodojin plays with the easy moral of the story of a dumb monkey grasping at a reflection of the moon. He shows an aware monkey at play with the illusion. In fact, the monkey is simultaneously *making* the moon, for his hand traces the circle. He creates the broken perfection of Zen practice as he draws an enso in water.

Every aspect of experience is of dependent nature. It depends on vast, unknowable conditions, and it depends on the process of consciousness. Something exists here and now, the illusion that we call life: your breath, the feelings in the palm of your hands, these words on paper, how you're feeling right now, this vast moment. But, since this illusion is simply the product of a torrent of habits of mind (or karma in the storehouse ripening) and countless other conditions we do not see, it does not exist. It is not what it appears to be to you. If you see it as existing you are grasping at the imaginary nature, and ignoring, or not seeing, the dependent nature. Each aspect of experience—from the whole field of your sensory perception to the tiniest mote of dust floating in the air—is subject to this analysis.

This verse upholds one of the central tendencies of Yogacara thought. It affirms that something is happening and denies that it's what you believe it to be. In particular, Vasubandhu here reminds us that the illusion exists. What are illusions for if not joyful engagement? Sometimes people claim that saying things are illusory means we will not or should not care about them. This does not reflect my experience. We naturally delight in and marvel at magic tricks. We walk into plays, movies, songs, and stories willing to be deeply moved or challenged. At the movies, people cry in the dark, or cringe at a shock. We create illusions and they transform us. We know that Wonder Woman isn't real, yet she inspires. We offer our whole selves to the experience of the illusions, the stories that artists offer. We can pour our whole selves more deeply into life when we realize that it exists as an illusion rather than something to be grasped.

To embody this teaching is to bring open-heartedness, creativity, and freedom into every aspect of our lives. One day while I was head cook at our Zen center, I realized the retreat activities were way behind schedule and all the food I'd carefully prepared was going to come out overcooked. I was seething. Then, I remembered that the executive producer of this whole drama was karma. What a show! A little smile showed up and I got back to the tasks of caring for the food. Suzuki Roshi tells of a time during World War II when folks in Japan were near starving. He managed to grow a few vegetables in the temple's patch of ground. Anyone could see he had barely enough. He shared his crop with people in the community, and people in the community began to share rice at the temple. He saw through the illusions of scarcity and aloneness, and with the people in his little town he planted a few quite wonderful seeds.

This teaching is for when you go for a walk, when you join a meeting, when you wash your hair, write a letter to the editor, listen to a speech, read a book, tell your stories, sit on the cushion, stand up from the cushion, face your teacher, read the news. This teaching is for all, and for freedom.

We stand at an easel before a canvas slashed with brushstrokes, with brush in hand. But we do not paint alone. This image depends on many hands. We stand on the bandstand. The music surges, it flows. Horn at our lips, what will we offer? Let us offer our deep listening, and respond to the call. Let us offer the notes that are true to us and that we want the world to hear. Something arises. The first rule of improvisation is "yes, and": to meet what arises with the whole self and offer creative response. We don't have to say yes to agree with the world, but we can say yes to acknowledge that we are creating it. Like the monkey in Kodojin's painting we can find a sense of play in which seeing and creating, perceiving and acting, and what is seen and what is created are not separate but are immediately present as experience—vivid and alive.

13

Nonduality Is Real

Since it exists as nonduality and is the very
Nonexistence of duality, the complete, realized nature
Is considered to have the characteristic
Of existence and nonexistence. ||13||

The complete, realized nature—what Buddhas see, the way things really are—exists as nonduality, but it also does not exist. This is because it is simply the absence of duality. Existence is dependent on duality; for something to exist it must not be nonexistent. Nonduality, the complete, realized nature, can be said to exist only because it also doesn't exist, otherwise it wouldn't be nondual!

These days many people are interested in investigating what racial whiteness is. In the Zen communities I'm connected with, we offer trainings in unpacking whiteness for white folks who want to understand their racial identities and how they are connected to the racism that has characterized the United States since its founding. One of the things we may study is the well-documented fact that the idea of races as bio-logically distinct classes of humans is less than five hundred years old. Further, the theory that there are biologically distinct races has been debunked in the scientific community. The racial dualities between white and Black, or white and Asian, is just a social construct, a group imagination; it is of imaginary nature. Sometimes when folks are exposed to this idea they leap to the idea that since race is not real, we're all one, and we should ignore race. Unity is surely a valuable concept for bringing people together, but if we want to liberate all beings from suffering, simply ignoring race isn't going to work.

When you begin unpacking whiteness and after you learn that race doesn't exist, you are encouraged to spend the rest of your time dismantling the impacts of race: your subconsciously embodied reactions and mental biases, white dominance in Western Buddhist communities, mass incarceration, white supremacy in almost every major institution in the United States, massive wealth disparities, and so on. The methodology of this work directly parallels the approach laid out in the "Treatise on Three Natures": to see the nonduality, but not let it congeal into oneness, to root the practice in mindfulness of body and emotions, and to recognize the illusion and to work for liberation within it. We are invited to stay flexible in our understanding even as we face the emotional turmoil of the work, for without mindfulness of emotions, we may burn out. We can hold to the knowledge that race isn't real, but that its impacts are very real for all of us. We can do this together, aware of the emotional challenges of the work. I've seen people doing it, and I believe you can.

So nonduality is not oneness, and it is important to distinguish between the two in order to avoid what psychologist John Welwood called "spiritual bypassing." Nonduality should not be a means of avoidance. It is clear seeing, flexibility, and joyful, compassionate engagement. In the *Avatamsaka* (*Flower Garland*) *Sutra*, a young man named Sudhana begins a quest to learn from an array of great teachers: princes, goddesses, bodhisattvas, young girls and boys, craftspeople, mendicants with matted hair, monks and nuns, and spectacularly generous queens. Each one propounds their attainment of staggering heights of awareness of nonduality, and then exhorts Sudhana to keep searching, for they are sure he can go beyond their attainment, and they must keep devoting themselves to their own distinct and diverse practices—to feeding people, meditation, freeing prisoners, offering healing touch, studying math, spreading flower garlands and glorious scents, teaching Dharma—in order to realize (make real) what they have attained. Their sense of completeness is profound, and yet they know that something is missing. They see the real, the nondual, and they know it's all illusion.

Nonduality here refers to both the nonduality of anything that we think is dual (anything we think exists or doesn't exist) but it also refers to the nonduality of subject and object. This nonduality is real and complete, and it's already here. You are already not you, and all the things you see are not things. The separations are just a bunch of ideas. You can't be alone, or apart, or a part. At the same time, this can be true only here in this moment where it seems like I am here and you are there. Nonduality, complete realization, is not somewhere else. This complete, realized nature may seem far off; I know that we often don't feel complete or realized.

> A monk asked Xuansha, "What is it, and why is it
>   so hard to realize?"
> Xuansha said, "Because it's too close."[21]

I recommend just sitting, every day, in a formal posture of meditation without any aspiration to attain anything or even to focus on an object. In Zen we call this objectless meditation, *shikantaza*. Tibetan mahamudra texts call it nonmeditation. Yogacara texts call it samatha or cessation. It really helps to have a teacher. Of course, I also recommend meditation methods that involve distinct focus on the breath, the whole body, emotions, or sounds, but it is good to take some time for just sitting with no object. You can bring this objectless activity to your daily life, too. You can walk just to walk, not to get somewhere else, sweep just to sweep, not waiting to be done, pour yourself into the wholeness of the activity. With practice we can learn to attend a meeting just to attend the meeting or plan just to plan. In the zendo, after zazen, we can stand still as others slowly rise on creaky knees to find their feet, as the teacher offers bows, as the rays of dawn and bird-songs slip through the cracks in the curtains. We don't have to stand there until it's time to go. We can just stand there. There is no waiting in Zen.

14

Oneness and Duality

Since an imagined thing is known as dual
But being one due to the absence of that duality,
The imaginary nature of the foolish
Is said to be both dual and unitary. ||14||

All is one. It has been said so many ways. So many people have emerged from profound spiritual experiences
with a powerful message of unity. Yogacara teachings,
being rooted in nondualism, affirm experience, but
deny that our interpretations of it are ultimate truth.
Realizing that we are all one can be helpful, but as
these teachings say, this is just another way of looking
at things.

Imagined things are known as dual. The sound of
the hammer falling again and again next door seems to
be something other than silence—and other than me.
The softness of the autumn sun on whispering leaves
outside my window seems separate from the bright,
white light of a midsummer day. I know that where I
am is different from where you are, that yesterday is

gone, and that tomorrow is yet to come. Despite this, sometimes I feel a profound sense of unity. Sometimes our sense of alienation dissolves. The ascribing of attributes to things pauses, and we are aware of the absence of duality. We may describe it as oneness when, after walking upstairs to meet the teacher during a meditation retreat, the mind's conditioned tendencies to divide soften thanks to hours of silence and meditation. Or perhaps this happens in a moment of profound intimacy with a forest, a prairie, a dying loved one, or a lover.

Our sense of being alien, alone, cut off, or unsupported is a key and profound driver for our suffering. The sense of being a separate self, which makes the world look other, arises with a heavy price. As this sense of alienation hardens, deepens, and dominates our experience, our suffering and that of those around us grows. In the moments of wrenching conflict with our loved ones, we should turn our attention to how separate we feel. When you are viewing a political opponent or someone from a different culture as profoundly alien, shine the light of your attention within and see what is happening in your heart and mind. The great Sufi poet Hafiz once wrote

> I have come into this world to see this:
> the sword drop from men's hands even at the
>   height

of their arc of anger
because we have finally realized there is just one
flesh to wound

I need this message when I want to control, judge, and dominate, and yet, oneness is not an ultimate truth. It's just another way of looking at things, an imagination. Hafiz was Muslim and I am not. He believed in God; I never have. Years ago, when I would wrestle with my spiritual understanding, an old Ojibwe spiritual friend used to say to me, "There ain't but one God, dude." I appreciated his desire to make me feel the wholeness and goodness of a unitary, universal God, but I also felt that he was denying my own beliefs and distinct worldview. Even as we develop some sense of the wholeness and oneness of everything, Yogacara teachings say we must uphold what the great Zen teacher Shitou called the "harmony of difference and sameness."

Audre Lorde was a Black lesbian essayist and poet with a profound awareness of her predicament as a person oppressed in an anti-Black, misogynistic, and homophobic culture. Her work shows a deep commitment to personal and shared liberation, and it has roots in the nondualism she found in the ancient Chinese divination text, the I Ching.[22] As she wrote in her famous essay, "The Master's Tools Will Never Dismantle the Master's House," "Difference must be not

merely tolerated, but seen as a fund of necessary polarities between which our creativity can spark like a
dialectic. Only then does the necessity for interdepen-
dency become unthreatening."

Oftentimes we cling to a sense of oneness to avoid
the messy reality of our interdependence. We try to
smooth over conflict by saying, "We're all just one
happy family!" We deny difference when we say, "Black,
white, brown, purple . . . doesn't matter to me!" Or, "I
think it's silly to tell people your pronouns." And,
"Women can lead just like men." But what if women
want to lead differently, in a way that is authentic to
their gender identity? Can I realize that my whiteness
affects how I view things and how I'm viewed? That
my bisexuality is not the same as straightness or gay-
ness? That people who cannot walk have different
access to my Zen center than those who can?

Throughout the Mahayana literature, which is
rooted in nondualism, we see the theme of how a
bodhisattva's challenge is *anupatitika dharma ksanti*,
learning to tolerate emptiness and everything's inherent ungraspability, which is rooted in interdependence.
Realizing oneness, or using the language of oneness
and unity, can help us cut through the imagination of
our division, alienation, and separation. Please, though,
be careful not to use it to avoid or deny the dynamic
reality of our difference, diversity, and interdependence, for these are the grounds of transformation.

They are the realm of liberation from suffering and healing of wounds both ancient and fresh.

I don't like to say folks are foolish, as Vasubandhu does in this verse. But I guess it's a nice reminder that we're all in the same boat, foolish, confused, working together poorly at times, well at others, trying to safely get to shore. We tear the sails, read the stars wrong, hoard and steal, and yet at heart, we just want to be well and are doing our best.

The Pang family are a trio of mostly mythical Zen teachers from eighth-century China. There is an unbroken thread in their teachings: the inseparability of their foolishness, wisdom, practice, and simple daily acts. Here is a poem from the father of the family:

> What I do every day
> Is nothing special:
> I simply stumble around.
> What I do is not thought out,
> Where I go is unplanned.
> No matter who tries to leave their mark,
> The hills and dales are not impressed.
> Collecting firewood and carrying water
> Are prayers that reach the gods.[23]

15

Life Has Arisen Like This

Since it appears to have a dual nature,
And being one as that is mere illusion,
The dependent nature
Is said to be both dual and unitary. ||15||

When you see the dependent nature of something, you're not seeing something different from what you see when you see its imaginary nature. In each case there is duality, and this duality is not real. However, this and the last verse show distinctions between how we view these two natures. To restate them: we *know* the imaginary is dual, but it isn't, we're wrong. On the other hand, the dependent *appears* dual, and we can be aware it's illusion.

As he sat in the Birmingham jail, Dr. Martin Luther King Jr. wrote, "I cannot sit idly by . . . we are caught in an inescapable network of mutuality." Dr. King's spiritual vision included the bars of the cell, the hard cots, the shared toilets, the dull moans of incarcerated bodies. This must be what he saw, he heard. We can imagine he felt all the pangs of the heart a person in such unjust subjugation can feel. In that letter from Birmingham Jail, we can feel his anger and frustration with "white moderates" who complained about his methods. Yet right there he saw that, "we are tied in a single garment of destiny." To see the dependent nature of things, we see the illusion that getting one thing, say a new contract for sanitation workers, integrated schools, or the Voting Rights Act, will resolve the great dependent mass of suffering in which we live. We see that, as it says in the *Dhammapada*, "victory begets enmity, the defeated dwell in pain, happy the peaceful live, discarding both victory and defeat."[24] When we see the dependent nature, we see there is no object that can be controlled or dominated; we see that our action is offered into an infinite web of interdependence. Victory is bound to defeat, and violence is bound to violence. On my altar I have a picture of Dr. King and Thich Nhat Hanh sitting together, with words from Dr. King below the image. It reads, "This is the unusual thing about nonviolence—nobody is defeated, everyone shares in the victory."

Dr. King poured his life into working for that new contract for sanitation workers, for the Voting Rights Act, for integrated schools; similarly, you can do your work and enact your life in a way that cares for and brings about beneficial change. And, you can do so with awareness of the dependent nature. As a white man in the United States, I am called to know that I am afforded safety, wealth, and power at the expense of women and people of color. Aware of my interdependence with these harms, I am called to dismantle the systems—and my own habits of body, speech, and mind—that create this privilege.

We can know that everything only *appears* as dual, and that the appearance of things as separate is an illusion. We can dissolve our tendency to think that getting away from something or holding onto something else will actually work to resolve the vast web of shared suffering we live in. Here in Minnesota in the winter we huddle inside and gripe, waiting for the warmth to come. As a nation, we wait for the next president. Each of us might hope to find the right one to love, or await a graduation, or for the workday or meeting to end. We wait and wait until we can get a new car, phone, patio, pizza—we wait for another thing to get, get rid of, or ignore. It doesn't have to be this way. We can see through the constriction and scarcity of this mindset and awaken to something greater.

To see the dependent nature is to have your view expand from the small and graspable, to the vast and free. You can see this right now in the rustling of autumn leaves, or the drone of the day's third meeting, in the hopeless argument with your teenage child, or the fiftieth time you've found yourself standing in a crowd chanting, "No justice, no peace," and while walking in a silent procession to stem the tide of environmental destruction. We can see that controlling things is an illusion and relationship is reality. I doubt Dr. King believed he would see the entire world living in beloved community during his lifetime, but this dream is alive though he is gone. Although injustice continues, I am so grateful to be held by, and move within, beloved communities of people honoring difference and working for a just and peaceful world. The freedom this verse offers is not somewhere else. It is freedom from the dual and the one, freedom to act with compassion for all. This freedom is already here, for everything is already of dependent nature.

16

The Taste of Freedom

Since it is the nature of dual existence,
And the singular nature of nonduality,
The complete, realized nature
Is said to be both dual and unitary. ||16||

The complete, realized nature is what is real, what is whole. It is the truth that buddhas see, and it is the very nature and essence of all dualities and everything that exists. It is one thing: the nonduality of anything that appears as dual. The liberation, peace, compassion, joy, and activity of Buddhist awakening is inescapably here and cannot be found elsewhere. It will not be found by getting rid of, ignoring, or avoiding, but by seeing what is here: this body, these sounds, these emotions, these very thoughts.

A monk asked Dongshan, "What is Buddha?"
Dongshan said, "This flax weighs three pounds."

This monk would have been immersed in a culture, a literature, and a physical environment that held Buddha to be something mind-bogglingly, transcendentally wondrous. He would have made daily offerings and bows to golden buddha statues, recited stories about buddhas liberating vast universes full of diverse arrays of people and gods. Yet when he asks Dongshan, "What is Buddha?" Dongshan directs him to embodied, dualistic, and discerning engagement with the present moment by caring for the temple's crops.

Dongshan is famous for being a founder of the Caodong (Soto) Chan school, and also for the burning question that drove his spiritual quest as a young monk. He'd heard a teaching that inanimate things preach the Dharma. He couldn't understand the teaching, but he couldn't dismiss it either. He poured himself into years of meditation, simple temple life, inquiry with teachers, and wandering in the mountains and fields. One day, while grieving a parting with his beloved teacher, Yunyan, and gazing at his reflection in a flowing stream, duality, oneness, and nonduality collapsed in the simple act of seeing. All the things you see, hear, smell, taste, and touch are showing you the Dharma, complete realization. The great Chan nun Xinggang once wrote a verse titled "The Alms Bowl":

How very elegant it is, with not even a single leak or hole!

When thirsty I drink; when hungry I eat, leaving
  not a crumb
I understand that once washed, nothing more need
  to be done,
Yet how many lost souls insist on attaching a
  handle to it.[25]

A simple begging bowl for food, complete. Eating, drinking, washing, all complete. Katagiri Roshin used to say "nothing extra." A handle? Not necessary. There is no need for control; everything is whole. Yet, this wholeness is the phenomenal dual world of activity.

One day Zhaozhou was sweeping.
A monk asked, "The master is a great worthy, why
  then are you sweeping?"
Zhaozhou said, "Dust comes from outside."
The monk said, "It's a pure temple. Why then is
  there dust?"
Zhaozhou said, "There's some more."[26]

Purity, dustiness, right here, just sweep. Zhaozhou is arguably the most revered and studied of Zen's founding ancestors, and his realization of freedom is essentially that there's dust; there's inside and outside; and when there's sweeping to do, you can just do it. In the *Uposatha Sutta*, the Buddha said, "Just as in the great ocean there is but one taste—the taste of salt—so in this Doctrine and Discipline there is but one taste—the taste of freedom." This is most commonly understood as freedom from suffering, but in Yogacara thought this freedom is bound to the fact that there are not things that can be controlled. Everything is always already free. Yes, there are all these things—hands, eyes, tears, rage, words, brooms, dust, bowls, and measuring cups—and they have one nondual nature: the complete, realized nature. This is why, after morning zazen at our Zen center, we pick up brooms and rags and attend to simple work; it is why the *tenzo*, or head cook, is one of the highest officers in a Soto Zen temple. If you have a life, you have the opportunity to do simple tasks, not to control or gain an outcome, but simply to do them as an enactment of your shared freedom.

If we care about liberation, if we want everyone to be free, there is tremendous power in realizing the liberation that is already here. On my altar I have a replica of the key to Nelson Mandela's prison cell on Robben Island. I have it to remind me of injustice, to remind me that the work to end apartheid mattered, that the work of liberation goes on. How can someone like Nelson Mandela, locked in a tiny cell for eighteen years, live with such energy to work for a better world, with such staggering magnanimity? How does Jarvis Masters, the Buddhist author and beloved counselor who has been on death row at San Quentin for the last thirty-five years, find the power to keep going with such compassion and strength amid such horror and injustice? I believe that they see more clearly what is right here. With practice, or with a sudden awakening, we can see that every moment, wherever you find yourself, is a moment of simple activity, that liberation is here within the dustiness and messiness of our shared lives. The complete, realized nature is not somewhere else, it is the essence of everything we see as dual, and it is merely their nonduality.

17

Suffering and Freedom

The imaginary and dependent are known
As the characteristic of affliction.
While the complete, realized is known
As the characteristic of purity. ||17||

From a Buddhist perspective, the three natures are different in the most important sense: The imaginary and dependent are characterized by affliction; the complete, realized nature by purity. Purity (*vyavadana*) is freedom from affliction (*klesa*) and what causes suffering. A central and repeated teaching of the Buddha is that he taught only suffering and the cessation of suffering. This is fundamentally about healing. This about caring about how we feel.

Vasubandhu introduced the term *laksana*, characteristic, in verse 10 and will use it in the next four verses to point out that the three natures are *not* different in characteristics, yet here he points out their fundamental differences. As usual, he applies nonduality to his own claims. The term *laksana* is associated with a basic teaching in Buddhism. Early Buddhist teachings invite us to see three laksanas, three marks, of all phenomena: impermanence, suffering, and nonself. Mindfulness teachings invite us to see the arising of phenomena and their passing away, their impermanence. The teachings ask us just to notice this breath, this pain in the lower back, this feeling of inexplicable joy, this sorrow, this thought, this moment of sunlight dappled on the grassy ground, as well as these phenomena passing. None of it remains, it all always passes, and even the sense of being one who observes has no fixed quality. As Dogen Zenji says in *Genjokoan*, "If you practice intimately and return to where you are, it will be clear that nothing at all has unchanging self."[27] Seeing impermanence opens the door to seeing nonself; we don't see fixed, lasting entities, but merely flux. As we do this we are invited not to ignore or evade suffering, the subtle, or not-so-subtle, sense of wanting things to be other than how they are. We are invited to really see it. Thus we begin to know the three marks.

In early Buddhist teachings we are instructed to see that nothing we are mindful of in this field of flux is our own self. When we really know this, there is no self that can cling to phenomena or suffer. The great Theravada monk Buddhaghosa wrote, "There is suffering, but none who suffers."[28] He is describing seeing the marks of suffering and nonself from an Early Buddhist perspective. When you see these, there is liberation, you are in nirvana, because there is not a "one who suf-fers." Put another way, *you* are not in nirvana; that's what makes it nirvana.

Thich Nhat Hanh consistently teaches the three marks in a way that is rooted in the three natures of Yogacara. He says that the three marks are imperma-nence, nonself, and nirvana. Nirvana replaces suffer-ing as an inescapable aspect of phenomena. In verse 31 of this text and in various Yogacara sutras these three natures are called the *laksanatraya*, three marks. Thich Nhat Hanh, like all Yogacarins, wants you to know that nirvana is already here. The imaginary nature, characterized by affliction, is this flux of impermanent phenomena we call life. The dependent is the fact that they have no self; they don't have self-nature for they are only dependencies. The complete, realized nature is nirvana. This is where buddhas live, where you live. The *Samdhinirmocana Sutra*, the first known Yogacara text, provides the earliest recorded definition of the complete, realized nature: "All phenomena are unpro-duced, unceasing, quiescent, from the start and natu-rally in a state of nirvana."[29]

These three natures are basic characteristics of all phenomena from a Yogacara perspective. The imaginary and dependent natures are suffering; the complete, realized is nonsuffering. The first two are associated with samsara, affliction, impurity, and duk-kha. The complete, realized is associated with nirvana, cessation, and liberation—with what the Buddha calls in one Pali sutra, "the truth . . . the peaceful . . . the deathless . . . the wonderful . . . the amazing . . . the refuge . . . the destination and the way leading to the destination."[30]

The imaginary nature is characterized by a sense of being a self that perceives things that are other. This sense arises from our karma—our habits of body, mind, and feeling—and produces grasping. The act of seeing things as other is an inherent act of grasping, and this grasping is tied to wanting to push away or hold on (desire and aversion), which is informed by the fundamental delusion that there are a self and others. This world of imagination and perceived alienation is where we live. This matters because what we feel and see and say and do in this imaginary field is where we know suffering. Please awaken compassion!

The dependent nature is suffering in that our suffering arises from conditions: you might eat a bag of chips to avoid your feelings, or you might think of someone as evil after they insult you. It arises even when you ruminate on a mistake. We are reaping the pain of thousands of years of shared conditioning such as patriarchy and othering, untold trillions of karmic acts of ignoring, belittling, violating, objectifying, pigeonholing. It adds up to where we are.

Many other Yogacara teachings say that the dependent nature is also nonsuffering. It occupies a middle space between the imaginary and the complete, realized nature. When we see what arises from conditions as real, we see the imaginary nature and grasp it as real, and we suffer. When we see what arises from conditions as mere dependency, we see the complete, realized nature—and find liberation.

The complete, realized nature is here, and it is the end of suffering. It is wondrous, free, and peaceful; it is the refuge and the path leading to the refuge. When there is nothing to grasp, there is no grasping. The complete, realized nature is simply that what appears to be things is not. You're not going to get something later, you didn't have something before. There is no you that can control or be controlled and no things you can control. You are not a victim of circumstances or of your habits. There is freedom now to act for the liberation of all, for this right here is the destination and the path leading to the destination.

18

Samsara and Nirvana Are One

Due to nonexistent duality nature and
That very nonexistence nature,
The complete, realized is said to be nondifferent
In characteristic from the imaginary. ||18||

The next four verses all address the fact that the complete, realized nature is identical to the imaginary and dependent natures. Their difference and their sameness are in harmony. These four verses each follow a logical formula: Due to an aspect of X, and a corresponding aspect of Y, Y and X are not different.

This verse says the imaginary is the same as the complete, realized nature because the complete, realized nature is simply the truth that the imaginary is not real. If we recall the last verse, we can see that this means that suffering and nonsuffering are inseparable: samsara and nirvana are one. Seeing the truth about samsara is liberation, but not liberation *from* samsara—rather, liberation that is inseparable from samsara.

American journalist Ida B. Wells was a cofounder of the NAACP. She was born enslaved, friends of hers were lynched, and she worked throughout her life to make a better world. She's best known for using the press to publicize lynchings. She saw how people ignored or denied the brutal violence being used to oppress Black folks, and she saw the power of turning toward the truth of suffering. She once wrote, "The way to right wrongs is to turn the light of truth upon them." Although she wrote this phrase in a particular and horrifying context, it bears a universal wisdom. The root of Buddhist teachings is to turn toward and to acknowledge suffering. This is the first noble truth. We know that we are in samsara and that suffering is vast, varied, and epochal, for we see (and are) those hearts and bodies that must bear it. This verse of Vasubandhu's invites us to turn this truth again to see that samsara and nirvana are one. Escape is not real, but peace is possible wherever we are. We can see the complete, realized nature in the imaginary, so the energy of our lives manifests compassion, joy, and peace for the benefit of all amid the suffering.

In Vasubandhu's *Mahayanasamgraha-bhasya*, he writes:

> All afflicted phenomena are called samsara and the nature of identitylessness of these afflicted phenomena is called nirvana . . . Bodhisattvas realize the identitylessness of

all phenomena . . . They see that phenomena
lack any nature and that the whole of samsara
is nirvana by virtue of the utter peacefulness
they perceive . . .[31]

The Dalai Lama lives in exile, as do hundreds of
thousands of his countryfolk. When he was young, his
home nation of Tibet was invaded by China, and it
remains occupied. Yet, even as he acknowledges the
suffering of his people and works for repair, pouring
his life into creating a more just and loving world, he
does it with such lightness, warmth, and humor! A
friend saw the Dalai Lama give a talk to several thousand people on a stage lined with dignitaries. Afterward, as he walked off the stage, the Dalai Lama looked
down and saw a napkin someone had dropped. He
bent over, picked it up, folded it, placed it back on the
table, and continued walking.

Although these verses seem so lofty, the vision they
propose so hard to attain, we can see actual people
manifesting the wisdom that we can be both happy
and at peace while we turn our hearts, bodies, and
minds toward healing our world. We cannot expect
or demand anyone to do this, but we can be inspired.
Look to your friends when they do this, and take
inspiration from them. The limits of this capacity
have yet to be found, and our world's need for them
is vast.

"Overturning of the root" is one of the central concepts of Yogacara. Thich Nhat Hanh calls it "transformation at the base," and some call it "revolution of the basis." It refers to a fundamental change in the alaya, or storehouse. Recall that the alaya is the aspect of our consciousness where the seeds of our cognitive, emotional, and behavioral conditioning are planted and bear fruit. In Vasubandhu's "Thirty Verses" he says, "In enlightenment it [*alaya*] is overturned at its root."[32] The process by which we are impelled and live in a world formed by habit can radically change. In the *Mahayanasamgraha*, overturning of the root is defined as "having abandoned the afflictions while not having abandoned samsara."[33] Afflictions are those qualities of mind that are painful and cause us to do harmful things. Samsara is this great web of beings making their way through life.

The promise of this tradition is that you can be deeply engaged in healing and not suffer or add suffering. We can learn to sit with ourselves in meditation or with a friend in conversation and see when suffering arises without compounding it. A therapist can learn to be radically present to suffering without being emotionally reactive or exhausted at the end of the day from setting their feelings aside. We can learn to be present to our children's suffering without needing to vent because we had to stuff away our own frustrations. This is not about avoiding feelings; it is about the possibility of becoming less reactive to afflictive emotions. I speak with people on a daily basis who are finding this kind of freedom through practice.

Vasubandhu says in the commentary *Mahayanasamgraha-bhasya*, "Fundamental change is attained through weakening the strength of the latent tendencies of the afflictions contained in the alaya-consciousness and strengthening the power that is their remedy." It's not that complicated, folks! When you plant seeds of wellness in the way that you respond to a moment, harmful tendencies are weakened and beneficial ones grow stronger. Practice matters, and practice is simply what you do. You are always practicing something. When there is rage, can you meet it with compassion? Can you care? When you are listening, can you simply listen? When there is hunger, can you give or receive food? When there is greed, can you simply see it and not take? I believe you can.

All the quotes from the *Mahayanasamgraha* I've offered are from a chapter called "The Relinquishment That Is the Result of This Training." The training comprises giving, ethical conduct, tolerance, energy, meditation, and wisdom, also known as the six *paramitas*, or perfections. What is the relinquishment? It is the relinquishment of nirvana. It is giving up escape and seeing that nirvana is here in samsara. It is finding the generosity, the engagement, the stillness, the motion, the compassion, and the freedom of nirvana, the complete, realized nature, here in this imagined, troubled world. The chapter ends thus:

When the knowledge of the sameness
Of samsara and nirvana has arisen,
At that point, in them, therefore
Samsara itself becomes nirvana

For that reason, samsara
Is neither abandoned nor not abandoned
Consequently, nirvana too
Is neither attained nor not attained.[34]

Can you trust what is here and now? When we imagine something else, somewhere else, or some other version of ourselves, each of those dualisms are illusions. Seeing that they aren't real, seeing that each thing is complete and real *as it is*, can be a door to a radical transformation. As Dogen says, you are already inside the door, "playing in the entranceway." Inside and outside meet here. Where you are going and where you are meet here. Woundedness and healing are inseparable. You cannot but meet them, for this is your life, the life of the world.

19

Already Buddha

Due to nonduality nature and
Nonexistent duality nature,
The imaginary nature is said to be nondifferent
In characteristic from the realized. ||19||

When I came to Buddhist practice, I was seeking something else. I sought an escape from the anguish I experienced. My therapists told me it was the anguish of trauma from the past reproducing itself. My psychiatrist told me my brain didn't process serotonin properly. My addiction recovery friends called it defects of character, self-will run riot. My Buddhist studies called it afflictive karma. All these ways of looking at it have their utility, and I am deeply grateful for all who have supported me in finding the wondrous, joyful existence of today. When we suffer, when we see the suffering of others, it is right to seek wellness, to seek something else. However, it is also true that there is not something else, that you and I are not, and cannot, be broken. For if there is brokenness, there must be a wholeness that is elsewhere; this is a duality, and duality is just a habit of mind.

The complete, realized nature is merely the nondualness of what appears as dual. As I walked a path of healing with therapists, psychologists, and friends who believed in the possibility of freedom, I listened to my Zen teachers. They told me, "You are Buddha," and I began to find a deep trust in the moment, a peace, joy, and compassion that had no other. Amid my own inner turmoil, the conflicts with my loved ones, the damaged society we live in, there arose an ineffable sense of nonopposition, dynamism, creativity, and cohesion. In the Zen telling, the Buddha became the Buddha when Siddhartha sat beneath a tree and watched the morning star in the dim dawning of the day. He placed his hand on the Earth and said, "I alone with all beings realize the way." Buddha is the realization of the nonduality of all things. This is why you cannot avoid being Buddha. Whether you know it or not, what is real and right here *is* Buddha.

One of Vasubandhu's students, the seminal Indian logician Dignaga, once wrote, "It is the naturally pure cognition of ordinary beings that is expressed by the term 'buddha.'"[35] Everything in your field of experience falls under Dignaga's definition of cognition, and it is all already nondual, pure of any obscuration or affliction. Zen texts call this "ordinary mind." What we mean by this is the whole of experience *right now*.

In the commentary *Mahayanasamgraha-bhasya,* Vasubandhu writes, "Natural purity refers to the essence of what is pure by nature, which exists as suchness. Since this exists as the general characteristic in all sentient beings, it was taught that all phenomena possess the tathagata heart."[36] Suchness, thusness, just this—the sound of my fingers on the keys, a van moving through my peripheral vision, small drifting snowflakes, a subtle sense of heartache—it is thus. The quality of thusness, unbound by our ideas about it, is shared by all sentient beings, phenomena, and experience. This is natural purity, the buddha heart.

In the Bible, Luke 17:21 says, "The kingdom of God is within you." This quotation is also the title of one of Leo Tolstoy's books, which later became a foundation of Gandhian nonviolence. It is based in the experience of the inseparability of the self from the boundless love of the divine. The nonviolent movements that have emerged in the last hundred years have been immensely powerful, but people have worked for the benefit of the world without using violence for millennia. It isn't necessary to have some special spiritual experience to manifest nonviolence, but there is power in realizing that infinite love is already here. It is the nonduality of what we see as dual. Knowing that there is no other that can be controlled and that domination only hardens our tendency to see a world of alienation changes us.

The Zen icon Hakuin begins the "Song of Zazen" with "All beings by nature are Buddha." He goes on to say, in Norman Waddell's translation, "How sad that people ignore the near / And search for truth afar: / Like someone in the midst of water / Crying out in thirst." We are here together. We can realize this more deeply by seeing what is right here: the feeling of cloth against skin, quiet sounds, unnamed emotions in a field of compassion, the taste of a bitter tea, our hands on a railing, our feet on the floor. It is always already thus.

20
Ain't No Thang

Due to the nonexistence of how it appears,
And being the reality of that very nature,
The realized is said to be nondifferent
In characteristic from the dependent appearance. ||20||

Imagine you've stopped at a cafe and ordered a cup of tea. Folks come and go, a familiar song or two floats by, and you do not find yourself with a cup of tea in your hands. You begin to tense up. You think, "Where's my tea?" Yet another song goes by in the humid air of the bustling cafe. With irritation in your heart and voice you flag the server, "You never brought my tea." The server, chagrined, steps away to make some tea. It would have been so helpful at the start of this process to remember that the tea in question, which is "yours," exists only in your mind. This might help you get a little closer to how things really are and to feel and pass to others a little less suffering. Dependent on conditions, this tea, which has never been brewed, appears to exist to me and appears to belong to me. When this nonexistent tea isn't here, I'm annoyed. I invite you to consider just how much of the suffering in your life arises from things, like this tea, that exist only in your mind. Consider the freedom available to you in seeing the reality of the nonexistence of that cup of tea you are waiting for.

When I worked in a restaurant some of my pals were keen to point out when there was no value to getting upset about something. They'd say, "Ain't no thang." They realized that for something to create suffering for you, you've got to make it into a thing.

It is probably harder to see how a cup of tea you are holding in your hand—warm to the touch, smooth, fragrant, floral, and when raised to the lips a bit bitter, a bit sweet—is also nonexistent, and how realizing this opens a space of vast, compassionate freedom. All the qualities of the tea, including how it appears to you, are dependent on conditions. If we focus on mental conditions as Yogacara texts usually do, we find the ideas that warm is different than cool, rough different than smooth, and bitter different than sweet. These comparisons, or dualities, manifest unconsciously to create a distinct object, an apparent thing, like a cup of tea. Using a more materialist analysis, we can say the cup of tea appears dependent on fuel for the heating, on a factory for ceramics, on a server to place the tea in the cup, on soil from which the tea was grown, on worms living therein, on the billions of microorganisms living around the roots of the tea plant, and so forth.

In order to see the cup of tea, we ignore or are ignorant of the absoluteness of its dependence. We do not see the totality. Anything we believe is a thing isn't ultimately real; it is utterly dependent, not separate. The entire universe and all your conditioning arrive to make it appear thus, but it's not a thing. Perhaps when you are experiencing anxiety, irritation, or anger, you can pause and recall one of my colleagues at the restaurant strolling by as I fumed about a customer who was nasty because I had forgotten to bring a cup of tea they'd ordered. Imagine them saying to you as they would to me, "It ain't no thang."

Practically and paradoxically speaking, developing vocabulary can help us see through all the categorizations by which the mind makes experience into a bunch of things. Developing concepts can help us go beyond concepts, or to use Dogen's metaphor, we can use a wooden wedge to remove a wooden wedge. Bird watchers learn long lists of songs and species, and often as they do so, develop a profound sense of the interdependence of birds, themselves, and their environment. They can find a capacity for deep peaceful presence. Rachel Carson, author of the ecological classic *Silent Spring*, not only had a deep knowledge of—and wide vocabulary for—birds, she also sensed their profound connection to the trees, the meadows, the insects, and the air. She found peace and a call to action in the heart of this relationship. These arose not separate from but dependent on subtle and highly technical descriptions of birds and birdsong. Her sustained discerning attention opened the door to her sense of wholeness and intimacy.

Being deeply aware of emotional states is one of the most powerful things a person can do if they are interested in promoting wellness, healing, and freedom from suffering. I've spent a lot of time sitting in therapy environments where there is a huge poster on the wall covered in words describing feelings: happy, sad, angry, despair, bliss, fear, restlessness, and so on. We are reminded in these places to be mindful of our emotions, and to describe how we feel. Developing a complex and thorough vocabulary for our emotional experience by talking with people about it helps us see our suffering and wellness, as well as what drives our actions and perception of our world. As we develop an emotional vocabulary, we learn to care about and to be sensitive to how we feel. This is mindfulness of emotions.

This practice is threaded throughout the *Satipatthana Sutta*; we are instructed to know when there is desire, anger, tranquility, restlessness, energy, rapture, sluggishness, and many other mind states. In Vasubandhu's "Thirty Verses," he points us toward awareness of fifty-five types of phenomena. Forty-one of them are emotional or affective. In terms of the three natures, this is about engaging the imaginary nature. We engage the I, the *manas*, that appears to exist, and turn its attention toward the emotional aspect of our experience, which appears separate. This is one of the most central practices Vasubandhu upholds in his teachings. I have seen it transform lives and relationships.

If we do this practice with patience, diligence, and commitment, healing and liberation will flow. As we learn to offer compassionate awareness to the array of emotions that arise within us, their power to drive us, and to reproduce themselves, will weaken. When we plant seeds of compassion and care, the seeds of suffering exhaust their power in the field of that compassion. This practice may also open up into something vaster. We may begin to see that an emotion that appears is merely a dependent arising. It's not a thing. We can't control it, we can't get rid of it, and it can't control us, destroy us, or overwhelm us. We can see that it is merely the way the universe happens to look through our limited, conditioned lens right now. We can see that the feeling, the circumstances, and the "I" that thinks it has or is the feeling is but the most ephemeral imagined thread within the vast fabric, the single garment, of what is whole, complete, and real. We can see that this moment is as real as it gets, because my friend, *it ain't no thang.*

21

Intimacy Is Transcendence

———————

Due to nonexistent duality nature and
Since how it appears is not its own nature,
The dependent is said to be nondifferent
In characteristic from the realized. ||21||

We can find the peace, stillness, dynamism, and compassion of the complete, realized nature here in our everyday lives by looking closely, by hearing deeply. We can use our intellects to challenge dualities that seem so real to us. We can cultivate a heart that knows connection rather than separation. We can dive into our activities and find the completeness of engaging in simple tasks. We can practice vipassana meditation and direct our discernment to the mysterious contents of our experience, and we can sit in samatha meditation and allow everything to simply be what it is. All of these involve a turning toward what is here, as a way to see through duality, through false appearances. All may help us realize that, as Zen master Shitou once wrote,

"The vast inconceivable source can't be faced or turned away from."

In the circles I travel, we often speak of "spiritual bypassing." This term was coined by the psychologist John Welwood to describe the way we try to evade the realities of our lives, often by holding to ideas of transcendence. Certainly all this talk of nonexistence can give us a way to use our intellect to create the illusion of escape from our own sufferings and those of our world. When we say, "It is what it is," or "It ain't no thing," or "It's all in your head," we may be using the mind to deny the heart. When my colleagues used to tell me "It ain't no thang," sometimes it would help me to let go, and other times it felt like a painful denial of the reality of my suffering. Yogacara teachings are not designed to paper over a mess; they are invitations to come closer to what is. In technical Buddhist terms this "what is" is called *dharmata, tattvartha*, or *tathata*, truth-ness, real thing, thusness.

The root teachings of Buddhism are about recognizing suffering and ending it. They relentlessly emphasize that we suffer because we think things last. They invite us to see this for ourselves by looking at our own experience. They ask us to look at "how things appear," and realize that they don't exist in that way. The *Satipatthana Sutta* asks us to dive into the sense of dualities between our self and other things, and this moment and other times. If we do this with energy and commitment, we will learn to see not only the dualities, but also that they are not real. The *Mahayanasamgraha* states:

> For those who are endowed with great means
> The afflictions become factors of awakening
> And samsara has the character of peace.[37]

In this verse, "great means" simply refers to long-term commitment to Buddhist practice. It is not by avoiding fear, desire, carelessness, irritation, or rage, but by recognizing them as factors of awakening that we can find peace in this vast shared world. If we want to realize our capacity to be of benefit, the best thing we can do is turn toward our bodies and our hearts—and then turn toward the world—with a sense that everything, no matter how painful, is an opportunity to awaken. Avoiding only hardens our sense of duality; turning toward, by contrast, plants seeds of seeing nonduality, thusness.

In the *Therigatha*, the record of verses by early awakened women, we find a verse by an old and infirm nun named Dhamma on the root practice of traveling and begging for food:

> I wandered for alms.
> I leaned on a stick.
> My whole body was weak
> and trembled.

Suddenly I fell down
and could see clearly
the misery of this body.
My heart was freed.[38]

Falling can be life-changing or fatal for the elderly. As a nun, Dhamma was impoverished by choice, but the body's frailty is a birthright of us all. Just in the moment of collapsing under the weight of her age and illness, her heart was freed. There was nirvana. Clearly seeing her embodied suffering marked her freedom from it. If we want to transform this world with its addictions, its losses, its endless desires, and its vast inequitable systems, poverty, and exploitation, let us take Dhamma's wisdom into our hearts. In this flux of changing conditions, the complete, realized nature is here. We find it when we see through the mirage that liberation is somewhere else, far from our suffering. To turn toward liberation is to turn toward life.

This does not mean you need to go find suffering and afflictions. There is peace in peacefulness, and joy in joy. When you see calm, joy, energy, and peace without believing that they are things you can hold onto, you plant seeds of calm, joy, energy, peace, and nonattachment. We can realize our dependence and completeness with a hug, a bow, a little smile, or by laughing like fools, or sharing silence. These seeds bear fruit for all. Everything that occurs in the heart is collective. Dhamma's awakening is here for us right now.

22

There Is a Path

For the purpose of growth in understanding,
These natures are often understood in stages,
From the point of view of conventions
and insight into them. ||22||

A young woodcutter with a load of branches on his back once heard a monk chanting the *Diamond Sutra* and suddenly awakened to reality. He then entered a monastery and was assigned to mill rice. This monk, Huineng, separated rice from chaff for years. One day, the abbot, who was looking for a successor, asked the monks to offer a poem expressing their understanding. The head monk, Shenxui, offered a poem encouraging diligent practice to clear dust from the mirror of mind so it can clearly show reality. Huineng, who was illiterate, asked a friend to write his poem down for him. It said that there's no mirror or dust, and everything is already empty, so there's no place for suffering to be. According to this legend, the abbot made the rice grinder Huineng his Dharma heir. He became a transmitter of Chan Buddhism and one of the most revered figures in Zen.

There is ongoing debate in Buddhist texts about whether awakening happens suddenly or gradually. Huineng's story was used to elevate the idea of sudden enlightenment. He awoke suddenly by merely hearing the *Diamond Sutra*. He expressed his enlightenment by saying there's no mirror to polish, no path of maturation. All that is so, but if there is no gradual path, why did he enter a monastery and spend years refining rice, carefully removing the grit from the good? Why write a poem, or pass a lifetime teaching Dharma? Throughout this text, Vasubandhu has shown the dual view that the complete, realized nature is what you are seeing now, and that you can *learn* to see it. Right now, you are awake *and* you can wake up.

The first Chan teachers were sometimes called Lankavatara masters. The *Lankavatara Sutra* integrates Yogacara with teachings on buddha nature. It emphasizes that the alaya is already of the complete, realized nature; the root of our consciousness is already free. Vasubandhu tends to emphasize that the alaya is of imaginary nature; we need to practice and plant seeds in order to affect a transformation at the root of consciousness. This will help us become peaceful, or mill rice, or write poems, and support our communities.

In the *Lankavatara Sutra*, Mahamati asks the Buddha whether our perceptions become clear gradually or all at once. Buddha answers in the affirmative:

> By degrees and not all at once. Like the gooseberry which ripens by degrees and not all at once, thus do tathagatas purify the stream of perceptions of beings' minds by degrees . . . or like a potter who makes vessels by degrees and not all at once . . . or like the Earth which gives birth to living things by degrees . . . or like when people become proficient in such arts as music or writing or painting by degrees and not all at once . . .
>
> Or just as a clear mirror reflects formless images all at once, tathagatas likewise purify the stream of perceptions of beings' minds by displaying pure, formless, undifferentiated realms all at once. Or just as the sun and moon illuminate images all at once, tathagatas likewise reveal the supreme realm of inconceivable wisdom all at once to those who have freed themselves of the habit-energy and misconceptions that are perceptions of their own minds. Or just as repository [alaya] consciousness distinguishes such different perceptions as the

realms of the body, its possessions, and the
world around it all at once, nishyanda buddhas likewise bring beings to maturity in
whatever realm they dwell all at once.[39]

This is how we realize the three natures: both gradually and all at once. The *Lankavatara* says all this is
done for us by buddhas. Their awakening is seeing that
awareness is not separate from anything. Because of
their vows for universal liberation, buddhas awakened
for you, because your awakeness now is not other than
their awakeness. In this and the next few verses,
though, Vasubandhu will emphasize that we wake up
gradually with practice.

Buddhism offers many descriptions of stages of
development: the eight *dhyanas*, the four foundations of
mindfulness, the ten stages of the bodhisattva, the ten
ox-herding pictures, and many others. My practice has
created gradual changes in how I act and feel. I see my
students grow in their ability to feel joyful, compassionate, and free. They grow in their understanding of
how to offer something beneficial. We grow together.
It has become common to see the earth as an object, a
lifeless thing from which we can take all we want. For
years people have been working to grow out of this
delusion. Last week I stood in the snow at the headwaters of the Mississippi and listened to Ojibwe elders
pray in the path of an oil pipeline bulldozer. They

prayed for "all my relations," as they gestured to the waters, the flattened trees, the standing ones, and all of us. We can gradually mature our ability to see the interdependence that is here, and to see completeness rather than scarcity.

The earth brings forth living beings by degrees and they are illuminated by the midday sun all at once. We can mature, by degrees, and awaken to the fact that this world is not an object. That you and I are not the Earth is just a way we look at things. We can learn to see the intimacy that is already here. So much fixing, judging, and extracting isn't helping. We can practice the art of letting the Earth give birth to us and our relations, which *are* the Earth. We can practice the art of letting the sunlight, the mind, and the moonlight illuminate.

23

Breaking the Chain

The imagined is conventional existence,
The other is the maker of conventional existence,
The third nature is the cutting off
Of convention, it is said. ||23||

Conventional views are so various. I recall an account of a Catholic church in Central America. In one alcove there was a statue festooned with corn. The priest explained to a visitor that this was *Jesus Cristo* the corn god, to whom the community made offerings for a good crop. Some Catholics, though, think this is heresy. When I was a teenager in Iowa, I did not let anyone know I was bisexual for fear of being ostracized or beaten. I could not imagine the kids I know now who take their same-sex dates to prom. There are cultures where people don't think of directions in relation to their own bodies, but in relation to the cardinal directions. They are not in the center of the space they occupy. Copernicus looked at the stars. He was conditioned by the conventional knowledge that the sun revolves around the Earth but saw that the earth revolves around the sun. He created conditions so that billions of people view the Earth and sky profoundly differently. Buddha repeatedly challenged the idea that people are born into a caste and that their roles and abilities are fixed by birth. He was explicit in stating that folks should be judged by their conduct, not their conventional status. Twenty-five hundred years later, Dr. King stood on the national mall and dreamed of a time when people would be judged not "by the color of their skin, but by the content of their character."

When we look at other cultures, they often seem strange, but of course our own is just as bizarre. Think of all that had to happen for bipedal humans to be living the way that we do and to develop all these assumptions! I like to think about what it would look like in an average Buddhist center if we didn't have shared conventions. It's not just that people might not offer a friendly bow to one another, or sit on cushions and chairs. People would be rolling on the floor, they'd be shouting, moaning, sleeping, chewing on the upholstery, reaching out and grabbing or gently stroking the walls, the floor, and the faces near them. The number of conventions that construct our moment-to-moment experience and actions are staggering.

Here is the first recorded definition of the imaginary nature, *kalpita svabhava*, which is translated below as imputational nature, from the seminal *Samdhinirmo-*

cana Sutra: "that which is imputed as a name or symbol in terms of the own-being [nature] or attributes of phenomena in order to subsequently designate any convention whatsoever."[40]

Concepts create ideas about the nature or characteristics of things, so that we "know" what they are. The language and symbols we live with contain countless assumptions. They form our conventional existence, the imaginary nature. When we are seeing only the imaginary nature, we are caught by and believe that these conventions are ultimate truths.

This is the section of this treatise where we are invited to see the three natures in terms of maturing our understanding. We are invited to see that these conventions are just the product of conditions, or of dependent nature. This means they are not ultimately true, and that they can change, or more precisely, that they are always changing. The idea of a fixed immutable culture does not withstand careful analysis. Culture is a process. We can create cultural forms that harm, such as anti-Semitism, Islamophobia, or the idea that the Earth is here to be exploited for human use. We can also create cultural forms that are beneficial: deep listening, attunement to interdependence, humility, the will to investigate and transform. We are always, in every moment, involved in the creation of the conditions that make the imaginary nature we share. Keep asking yourself: What seeds are we planting? What is the quality of heart and mind that I am offering to create our collective imagination?

The complete, realized nature is the cutting off of conventions, *vyavaharasamuccheda*. Other translators call this freedom from conventions. Progressing along the path of liberation is about seeing past these conventions, letting them die away, and being free from them. In the early first millennium, most Buddhist monks followed a strict code of conduct, living homeless on the outskirts of towns and only entering to beg for food, never touching money, avoiding all worldly affairs, and meticulously avoiding the temptations of sex and intoxicants. Monks and nuns were revered and considered spiritually superior to lay folks. The *Vimalakirti Sutra* is the story of a lay person of profound wisdom who teaches a crowd of the most venerated monks, arhats, and bodhisattvas. He relentlessly challenges convention:

> In order to be in harmony with people he associated with elders, those of middle age, and with the young, yet always spoke in harmony with the Dharma. He engaged in all sorts of businesses, yet had no interest in profit or possessions. To train all living beings he would appear at crossroads and on street corners, and to protect them he participated in government . . . To develop children he

visited all the schools. To demonstrate the evils of desire, he even entered brothels. To establish drunkards in correct mindfulness, he entered all the cabarets.[41]

As Vimalakirti challenged Buddhist conventions, I challenge the conventional idea of "the evils of desire." Although misusing sexuality can cause terrible harm, the shaming of sexual desire is harmful, too. Honoring the power and beauty of sexuality opens the door to a more beneficial engagement with it. Shaming sex workers is not helpful either. So yes, Vimalakirti, thank you for walking through the door, but we can keep entering forbidden chambers and meeting everyone where they are. No one should be left out.

So much great art is rooted in the understanding that we can be more free by cutting through convention: Miles Davis's relentless innovation, Virginia Woolf's stream-of-consciousness novels, Andy Goldsworthy's immersions in the natural world, Frida Kahlo's fantastic self-portraits . . . I recall a performance called "Art is . . ." by Lorraine Grady. During Harlem's African American Day Parade, a group of people wearing white and a crew of photographers accompanied a float. They carried ornate gilt picture frames, like you might see around a painting by Vermeer or Matisse. They held the frames up to the folks in the crowd and took pictures of them. In the photographs, people's faces show the joy of participating, of being seen, of being the subject of the art. In one photo, a woman looks through the golden frame and right into your eyes. Who is the subject? Who is the object?

So much Buddhist literature emphasizes seeing through conventions: There's the dazzling imagery of the *Avatamsaka Sutra*, where interdependence is described so relentlessly that our conventional minds melt into the telling, as well as Nagarjuna's precise and logical arguments that cut through the believability of any proposition whatsoever. The *Dhammapada* says, "If you want to reach the other shore of existence, give up what is before, behind, and in between. Set your mind free and go beyond birth and death." Time, space, birth and death, and our centrality in any of it are all merely conventional ways of seeing. The *Dhammapada* also says, "Follow this path and practice meditation, go beyond the power of Mara [lord of death]."[42] The path of ethical conduct and meditation leads far beyond conventions. You have the capacity to see that they are all merely created by conditions, to see through them to a deeper freedom, a freedom for all beings, for everything, for you.

24

Nonself, No-self, and Nondual

First one understands the dependent,
A dual nonexistence.
Then one understands the merely imaginary there,
Nonexistent duality. ||24||

Here Vasubandhu upholds two ways of understanding the dependent nature of things. One is from the Early Buddhist tradition and the other from the Mahayana. The *Mahayanasamgraha* calls these two ways "realizing personal and phenomenal identitylessness." Reams of Buddhist texts argue about which of these is correct. Yogacara integrates them while valuing their differences.

Early Buddhist literature teaches that all things arise dependent on conditions in a twelvefold cyclic chain: ignorance, consciousness, karmic formation, name and form, six senses, contact, sensation, craving, clinging, becoming, birth, old age and death, and back to ignorance . . . Each one leads to the other—and around and around we go. Ignorance, emotions, what is perceived, birth and death, and coming into being and passing away all depend on one another. These teachings say that by seeing this flux we can see that there is never anything happening within it that is our own self. Everything is nonself. When we realize this, we have dispelled ignorance. Thus the twelvefold chain is broken. When there is no ignorance, there is no consciousness, no karmic formation and so forth. Thus we see the unconditioned, the deathless; we see that there is no I, no self, that can suffer. In these teachings, "understanding the dependent" is breaking the twelvefold chain and seeing that everything is nonself.

Mahayana teachings emphasize that all phenomena have no self of their own. Each thing of any kind—smells, sounds, bodies, fears, words, thoughts, actions, leaves, squirrels—arises dependent on conditions. It is already true that nothing has independent existence. When we understand the dependent nature, nothing that we perceive exists: It is only the ignoring of infinite conditions that makes it seem like it does. We are left with no ground to rest on and nothing which can rest, and it is here that we realize liberation, a liberation like free falling. Vasubandhu's *Mahayanasamgraha-bhasya* states: "Bodhisattvas . . . realize both kinds of identitylessness—that of persons and that of phenomena . . . they become established in a place where they can relinquish afflicted phenomena and yet do not abandon samsara. This fundamental change that promotes both the bodhisattva's own welfare and that of others is vast."[43]

This verse says that to understand the dependent nature is to see that—as Early Buddhist teachings say—everything is nonself, or as Mahayana teachings say, all things have no self. We can come to see this "dual nonexistence," or the nonexistence of the self and of the other. Seeing the nonduality of self and other leads us to understand the imaginary nature. Vasubandhu presents these as a developmental path, as if one realization leads to the other, but in my experience folks realize these in various ways. For example, they might become less defensive as they realize nonself. They may be less demanding and controlling as they realize no self. You might find them happily gazing at a squirrel running along a high wire or more willing to intervene, with nonviolence, where there is harm as they realize the nonduality of self and other.

The *Yogavibhaga* is lost to time and exists only in quotations in other texts, such as this one, the *Mahayanasamgraha*:

Bodhisattvas in meditative equipoise
See that images are mind—
Through putting an end to the notions of referents,
They determine them as their very own notions.

Thus, the mind dwells on the inside.
They realize that the apprehended does not exist,
Thereby realizing that there is no apprehender
    [either].
Therefore, they are in touch with the
    unobservable.[44]

This is a distinctly Yogacara method for understanding dependence through meditation. We can
slow down enough to see that nothing in our field of
experience is other than our experience of it. For
example, try resting your attention on your body to
settle the mind. Close your eyes and place your fingertip on this book, and your attention on the feeling in
the fingertip. Now, investigate the difference between
the awareness of the sensation, your fingertip, and the
book. Then, try to locate what is observing these. This
and similar practices can dissolve the sense that there
are things outside of experience, or as we say in Yogacara, mind. We can realize that things as we experience them are dependent on our awareness of them. If
the "things" are dependent on our awareness of them,
then we will also realize that our awareness is dependent on the things. Awareness is awareness of something. As we realize that things depend on mind and
mind depends on things, we realize that there is nothing apprehended, and there is no apprehender; there is
dual nonexistence.

When we understand this, we understand the imaginary nature. We understand that it is merely this nonexistent duality. We can see through this sense of being a self that constantly needs to hold things or push them away. This may happen suddenly or gradually. We can deepen our understanding of this by studying and thinking, by practicing meditation, by pouring ourselves into our activities—by feeling our way toward it. I encourage you to find some trust in the process. As Vasubandhu says in the "Thirty Verses," "When there is nothing to grasp, there is no grasping."

25

Right View: Both/And

Then one understands the realized,
The existence of the nonexistence of duality,
For then it is just thus—
It is said to be and not to be. ||25||

In the last verse, we were offered a progression of understanding. First we see that the self and objects of observation don't exist because they are only dependencies. That helps us to see that the duality between ourselves and other things doesn't exist. In this verse, Vasubandhu says that by seeing in these ways, we can know what is real—what exists. He affirms this in two ways: One is precisely logical and philosophical, the other more evocative. Let's consider the first of these now.

Recall that in the *Kaccanagotta Sutta* the Buddha teaches that right view is not seeing that things exist or don't exist. Much Mahayana literature says that neither of these polarities are possible or real. In the Pali *Aggi-Vacchagotta Sutta*, we find an argument called a tetralemma, or fourfold negation. In the sutta, Vaccha-gotta asks the Buddha if after realizing nirvana one will be reborn. The Buddha responds that it's not correct to say "will be reborn," it's not correct to say "will not be reborn," it's not correct to say "will be reborn and not reborn," and it's not correct to say "will neither be reborn nor not reborn." All possible dualistic propositions are negated, nothing is affirmed. This style of argument becomes common in Mahayana literature.

In this verse, Vasubandhu takes a different logical route and affirms that nonexistent duality exists. There is something real, the nonexistence of duality, so what is real "is said to be *and* not to be." (Emphasis mine.) Rather than a logic of negation—neither/nor—Vasubandhu uses a logic of affirmation—both/and. The complete, realized nature of things is that they are not things, *and* they are just thus.

Mahayana literature emphasizes the negative approach by referring to things as empty, and the positive approach when using the terms *thusness* (tathata), *suchness*, or *as-it-is-ness*. This verse says when we understand the real, it is thusness. There is something happening here but you don't know what it is. There is no you, no what it is, and no happening: There is only knowing. And, there is no knowing—it's just this. Words fail, but we try, and we point to a central pillar of Yogacara: the affirmation of (for lack of a better word) experience. Something is happening, and everything that seems real about it isn't. When you understand this you know thusness, but of course it's always already thus.

Yogacara is generally associated with this both/and approach, and the other great Mahayana school, Madhyamaka, with neither/nor. The negative approach uses our capacity for logic to cut through our alienation. The affirmative language of thusness is used to evoke the experience of interdependence. This affirmative flavor opens the door for what will be a great flowering of Dharma in the form of the *Avatamsaka Sutra*, and the Huayan school of Buddhism in China. In the Flower Garland school, dependency is not simply used to show that things don't exist as separate; it is used to celebrate the wondrous display that emerges from this vast web of dependency. Here is a passage from the *Avatamsaka Sutra*:

> Without discerning any coming from anywhere on the part of the buddhas, without discerning any going on the part of my own body, knowing the buddhas as like a dream, knowing my own mind as dreamlike thought, knowing the buddhas as like a reflection, knowing my own mind as like a vessel of clear water, knowing the buddhas as like magically produced forms, knowing my mind as like magic, knowing the nature

of voices of the buddhas as the reverbera-
tion of the sound of echoes in the mountains, knowing my own mind as like an echo
I realize, I am mindful, that all enlightenment principles of bodhisattvas are based
on one's own mind . . . that all enlightening
practices, all development and guidance of
sentient beings . . . spiritual communions
with the cosmos, and knowledge of subtle
communions with all the ages, all are based
on one's own mind.[45]

Every moment of awareness or experience, is merely
mind. It is merely an echo or reflection of the whole
universe and of awakening. It is the only ground of
realization. The great Zen teacher Hongzhi channels
Huayan teaching when he writes, "Directly arriving
here you will be able to recognize the mind ground
dharma field that is the root source of the ten thousand
forms germinating with unwithered fertility. These
flowers and leaves are the whole world."[46]

We are invited through this path of affirmation to
arrive here where it is thus and where we are, but with
our ideas of separation dissolved into an ocean of
interdependence. In the final chapter of the *Avatamsaka Sutra*, the "Gandavyuha," we find story after story
about a fantastically diverse array of people and
beings engaging in all kinds of practices for the good

of those around them. Monks, nuns, boys, girls, queens, princes, merchants, mathematicians, prisoners, goddesses, and bodhisattvas all offer teachings to the pilgrim Sudhana. They provide food; they teach; they give healing touch; they create beautiful arts; they dispel fear; they free prisoners. Each has their own approach to liberation based on their capacities and relationships. Each one humbly invites Sudhana to continue traveling to find someone wiser and more kind than they. It is no wonder that Thich Nhat Hanh so often refers to Yogacara and the radical emphasis on interdependence in the Huayan as he creates Engaged Buddhist teachings. For those of us who want to celebrate the vast diversity and possibilities for freedom and healing in this world, here is an invitation. Arrive here, put down everything you know, and see what is real.

26

Nothing to Hold Onto

The three natures have the characteristic
Of nonduality, ungraspability,
Due to nonexistence, not existing like it appears,
And being the nature of that nonexistence. ||26||

The three natures share nonduality and ungraspability. This verse represents a shift in the text. The last verses have been looking at how we can mature and understand the three natures over time. They give us the idea that we can progressively figure out the three natures, grasp or attain them, and thus complete our path. This verse is a reminder that the path of liberation is not about getting something that you can hold on to. Healing is an ongoing process.

The three natures are ungraspable, *alabhya*. *Alabhya* can also be translated as "unobtainable," "unknowable," "unattainable," and "unlocatable." In order to be gotten, known, attained, or located, something must be a thing separate from other things, but the three natures are all nondual. The previous two verses are about how we can come to understand the three natures, and this one reminds us that what we come to understand is that they are beyond comprehension. I know for many folks that this is confusing, or perhaps frustrating. Another common definition of *alabhya* is "difficult." The three natures are difficult. I recall an old story about the Pang family:

> Layman Pang was sitting in his thatched cottage one day, studying the sutras. "Difficult, difficult, difficult," he suddenly exclaimed, "like trying to store ten bushels of sesame seed in the top of a tree."
>
> "Easy, easy, easy," his wife, Laywoman Pang, answered. "It's like touching your feet to the floor when you get out of bed."
>
> "Neither difficult nor easy," said their daughter Lingzhao, "It's like the teachings of the ancestors shining on the hundred grass tips."[47]

It may seem difficult, *and* you may find complete simplicity in embodied activity, *and* you may see that the Dharma is just the apparent flowering of the world. All of these are part of the process. In the *Diamond Sutra* we find this verse:

> Because the dharmas that the Buddha expounds are in all cases not some thing that

can be acquired, not something that can be expounded. They are not dharmas, and they are not not dharmas. Why do I say this? Because all the wise and holy ones in all cases deal in an unconditioned dharma that is expressed in terms of the conditional.[48]

Dharma with a capital "D" means "truth," "teaching," or "reality"; *dharma* with a lowercase "d" means "phenomena." In this quotation those meanings are collapsed. The teaching and what it is about are inseparable: The truth, reality, phenomena, and teaching cannot be grasped. We are invited into the process, to practice with their ungraspability, to find our freedom not by shoring up our defenses or creating certainty, but by engaging with flux.

My teacher's teacher, Shunryu Suzuki, frequently spoke of the importance of doing Zen practice with "no gaining idea." In particular he emphasized that zazen, sitting meditation, was to be done simply to do zazen, not to get, gain, attain, fix, or understand something. It can be hard to settle into this way of sitting meditation, but if we commit to it we may notice that it shows up in other aspects of our lives. We may find that we see the understanding of the three natures arising. We may realize we are always cocreating the world with whatever is happening and whoever is with us, and we may realize a profound peace, joyfulness, and completeness as we do it. I do not hope we figure out the meaning of the "Treatise on Three Natures." I encourage us all to dive into the study itself as a practice of liberation.

Number-two pencil in hand, crayons at the ready, at my small Formica-topped desk, I was taught that brave men created the United States because they wanted to be free, and this is why we had freedom. They figured out what freedom is, they wrote it down, and they fought to gain it. However, I later learned that many of these same men enslaved Africans. In this country I still hear about how we are free. I am grateful to not live in a colony ruled by a hereditary monarch on another continent, but people in the United States are still bound in countless ways. Believing that we can figure out or gain liberation is part of the problem. These verses invite us to see it as a process. As the civil rights icon John Lewis once said, "Democracy is not a state. It is an act." Liberation is something we do now. Three natures teachings tell us that we do it in the midst of our illusions. They reveal that we are always collaborating with the entire universe, and that we are never separate from this process. It is never something else.

Earlier this year, I was on the planning committee for an Earth Day event hosted by Minnesota Inter-faith Power & Light. All involved were deeply concerned about the climate crisis and its disproportionate impact on Black, brown, and poor people, and about an oil pipeline planned to run through the serene and treaty-protected headwaters of the Mississippi River, home of the Anishinaabe people. The organizers were constantly attending to the lived experience of the people in the group. They listened, cocreated, and sensitively brought in a diverse array of voices to make offerings at the event. There were specific actions we invited folks to take part in, and we set out long-term goals, but I felt that together we never lost sight of the fact that the path would be long, would extend far beyond our lives into the lives of our ancestors, and beyond the blip of time where humans will dwell on this planet. Our group included Muslims, Jews, Christians, Buddhists, and practitioners of Indigenous traditions. We didn't talk about planting seeds in the alaya, but we knew that our work was about how we were together. We honored ourselves and each other in each moment, and planted seeds of nonviolence, mindfulness, compassion, energy, and joy. I felt held in a shared sense that we were healing as people and as communities, and that we were encountering, one foot after the other, a shared path of liberation.

27

The Illusory Elephant

Just as an illusion produced by an incantation
May appear to be an elephant,
A mere form is there,
But the elephant is truly no elephant. ||27||

Here begins one of Vasubandhu's most famous teachings: the simile of the illusory elephant. This simile points out that we already know we perceive things that aren't real. Remembering this opens the door to seeing how powerful this tendency is. Being mindful of this tendency can deepen our humility, our commitment to Buddhist practice, and our understanding of the three natures.

Vasubandhu refers here to what seems to have been a familiar experience for people of his time; in the Pali Canon the Buddha makes a similar comparison as well.[49] A roadside conjurer, like a contemporary street-corner magician flashing a deck of cards, would utter a mantra or incantation. (I don't know any ancient Indian incantations, but I imagine they would say something equivalent to "Abracadabra!") The audience would gasp as an elephant appeared before their eyes. Imagine what would arise in the rapt attendees: fear, wonder, awe, a desire to touch it or to run away. All the emotions, thoughts, and actions, all the karma that come with seeing an elephant appear right in front of you might arise, but there wasn't really an elephant. After a minute or maybe after a few years of experiencing these conjurings, folks would realize that a conjured elephant is an illusion. They would know it looked like an elephant, but it wasn't an elephant. Today, we have magicians who can saw people in half, fly, and produce rabbits from hats. David Copperfield made the Statue of Liberty disappear! M. C. Escher drew a staircase that always goes up. *Abracadabra!* We know, generally speaking, that these are illusions, and we can enjoy being tricked. The point here is to recognize that we see things that don't exist. This verse appeals to our common sense about what we experience in order to open the door to challenging our commonsense views.

Here, Vasubandhu subtly refers to the degree to which our experience is conditioned by language. It is a mantra, words, which invoke the false image. The earliest Yogacara texts, particularly the *Samdhinirmocana Sutra*, emphasize the way language forms our false perception of the world. We don't see the world, but an array of imputations. This is a good reminder of two things: First, our words matter. You can transform how you view the world by changing how you talk and think about it. For example, try talking about gratitude several times a day for a month and see what happens. Second, if we want to get closer to the truth we should practice letting go of words. This is one of the many reasons Buddhists value silent retreat so highly. They help us fully feel our hands on a slippery plate in warm sudsy water, or know our breath, sense the thumb tips gently touching and hear the rising birdsong, feel sensations roll across our soles with a single step, taste a single blueberry, notice each leaf of grass and passing shadow.

Visualization practices are used in many schools of Buddhism. They help us remember that we can experience things that are not real, and they help us condition our minds by planting beneficial seeds. In *metta* practice, we visualize people and send them loving thoughts. To cultivate compassion in *tonglen* practice, we visualize people and imagine their suffering as smoke; we don't push it away, but breathe it in as our own. With Buddha visualization, we learn to see all the marks of liberation, to feel the joy of the presence of Buddha, and to realize that it is inseparable from our own mind.

Scientists studying visual perception investigate cases where we see things that aren't real, such as optical illusions. From this, they question whether we actually see anything real or true at all. Some scientists who study perception have brought forth the idea that we cannot perceive reality. Cognitive psychologist Donald Hoffman writes, "Perception is not a window on objective reality. It is an interface that hides objective reality behind a veil of helpful icons." He also wrote, "Space, time, and physical objects are not objective reality. They are simply the virtual world delivered by our senses to help us play the game of life." Neuroscientist Anil Seth argues, "Perception and hallucination have a lot in common. You could say that we're all hallucinating all of the time, and when we agree about our hallucinations that's what we call reality." These are by no means universal views among people in the field of perceptual, cognitive, or neuroscience, and their arguments are more complex and detailed than the quotes above can capture. I should also add that none of these folks suggest that what we perceive doesn't matter.

I first started learning about post-traumatic stress disorder when I was in high school, researching what my Vietnamese friends call the American War. The challenges U.S. veterans of the war experienced when they came home to the States were wrenching, as was the fact that I could find so little information about the impacts on the people of Vietnam. I recall reading about veterans back home in the United States diving to the ground or crouching under tables at the sound of fireworks or a backfiring car. They heard the sounds of impending death, of mortars and gunfire. I learned that for many veterans, part of recovery was realizing that the emotions they experienced when they heard a bottle rocket must be cared for, that the gunfire they imagined was not real, and that they could create conditions so people would not have to suffer similar trauma. In future chapters we will explore more deeply how the current understanding of trauma aligns deeply with the Yogacara approach to healing.

We can begin to realize, acknowledge, and be mindful of the fact that we see, hear, feel, think, smell, and taste things that aren't real. This can help us to investigate ever more deeply our delusions. What else are we misperceiving? Realizing our delusions, we will open the door to freedom and to a deeper awareness of what we can do to be of genuine benefit.

28

Learning the Trick

The imaginary nature is the elephant,
Its appearance is the dependent, and
The nonexistence of the elephant there
Is said to be the complete, realized nature. ||28||

Here is one of the simplest ways of describing the three natures you will find. Dependent on mental conditions we perceive something: an elephant, for example. The elephant is thus imaginary. The complete, realized nature is that the elephant isn't real. This means that what we do, think, and feel are of utmost importance because they create the conditions for what we will experience. It means that everything is interdependent and collective. And it means that what is complete and real—what buddhas know—is already how things are. We cannot acquire or avoid it, but we can shed the anguish, desire, and aversion of our reactions to it.

In the *Vimalakirti Sutra* the great Early Buddhist arhat Shariputra, a man, challenges a goddess based on his understanding that women cannot become buddhas. He sees being a woman as a limitation.

> *Shariputra*: Goddess, what prevents you from trans-forming out of your female state?
>
> *Goddess*: Although I have sought my "female state" for twelve years, I have not yet found it. Rever-end Shariputra, if a magician were to incarnate a woman by magic, would you ask her, "What pre-vents you from transforming out of your female state?"
>
> *Shariputra*: No! Such a woman would not really exist, so what would there be to transform?
>
> *Goddess*: Just so, reverend Shariputra, all things do not really exist.[50]

The goddess used the practice of investigating an aspect of herself—femaleness—to realize nonself and no self. Femaleness is not herself, and it is not locatable as a distinct, boundaried, lasting thing. It is a flux of ideas. She finds freedom by looking deeply, and she uses the metaphor of magical creation to melt the hardened categories of identity that Shariputra holds, categories by which his dominant status as a man is upheld. At the same time she teaches him about the liberatory possibilities of seeing through all things. She doesn't need to transform herself from her female state to find the truth, peace, and freedom of a buddha.

There are other similar exchanges between women and men in Indian Mahayana and Chan literature. Many other sutras, particularly Prajnaparamita texts, emphasize the method of cutting through ideas of identity.

However, there is also a great deal of literature across Buddhist traditions that affirms the importance of our identities, our categories, our things, and our shared and imagined world. In the *Vimalakirti Sutra*, after the exchange above, the goddess proves her point. She transforms herself into Shariputra and Shariputra into herself. Then she transforms them both back, quite content, it seems, to remain in female form.

In the Pali Canon we find the story of Mahapajapati, the first woman to ask Gautama Buddha for ordination. Although he had often taught that women were fully able to attain nirvana, he repeatedly refused to ordain her because he did not ordain women. Mahapajapati gathered together many women who wished to enter the order. They shaved their heads and took up the homelessness, poverty, and practice of the Buddha's monks. They began to follow Gautama Buddha around the country as he wandered, practicing just as he did. This, I believe, is the first recorded instance of group nonviolent resistance to inequity. Eventually the Buddha relented, and ordained Mahapajapati and many other women. Their poems, the *Therigatha*, is the earliest known collection of women's literature in the world. In it, women teach Dharma and talk about their lives in ways that distinctly relate to their identities as women. Although the Buddhist tradition is pervaded by patriarchy, there are many accounts of women valuing their identities and the particularly female ways of being and teaching Dharma.

In this teaching, gender, like all things, is merely a way of seeing. It is not an ultimate truth or real, lasting object. We may realize that we are always involved in co-creating what gender will mean for us, and we may find and learn of new genders, new ways to affirm identities, and to see through division.

In *Gabyo*, Dogen Zenji affirms the great Zen teaching that "a painting of a rice cake does not satisfy hunger."[51] An illusory elephant cannot give you a ride to the grocery store. As long as we seek to satisfy our needs with things of imaginary nature, the cycle of samsara will go on. For example, my maleness, in our patriarchal society, provides me unearned access to safety, wealth, and power, but does not actually free me from suffering. Later in that essay Dogen contradicts himself: "There is no remedy to satisfy hunger other than a painting of a rice cake." The only way I can practice awakening from patriarchy is as a male human being. It is here within this imagination, this moment of phenomena painted by the conditioning of mind, that healing and liberation are possible. Dogen says, "Because the entire world and all phenomena are a painting, human existence appears from a painting, and Buddha ancestors are actualized from a painting." I have seen mounds of perfectly good food thrown away even as people in my neighborhood go hungry. We can imagine something better so that people don't go hungry. We are, my friends, already creating the world together. The liberation that Buddhism offers is an activity; it is the process of shaping consciousness right now.

29

Trauma, Perception, and Healing

The false imagination thus appears
From the root mind as dual.
The duality is utterly nonexistent,
The mere appearance is there. ||29||

When I first came to Zen practice, I was also under-
taking several years of therapy for post-traumatic stress
disorder. I began to shed old fixed views and obsessions. I began to heal. I began to believe that the rage,
the terror, the despair, and the overpowering shame I
experienced were not happening because I was a bad
person. I began to believe that they were not necessary
components of myself or necessary fuel for my work as
a musician. I began to let go of the idea that the harm
I had experienced was my fault or insignificant. I began
to see that all the harm I had created was my respon-
sibility but not my destiny. I discovered that I was not
clearly seeing the things and the people I feared, and
at whom I raged. The process of this awakening was

wondrous and often very painful. At the very root of it was the understanding shared by my Buddhist teachers and therapists that my feelings, thoughts, and view of the world were arising due to a collection of past and present conditions. I suffered and caused so much harm because of habits of thought, emotion, and embodiment, but they were merely habits—and habits can change.

This verse reiterates that what we generally believe to be real arises from the alaya. It arises from our habits of perception, emotion, thought, and action. It is the fruit of karmic seeds. In the United States, there is a growing focus on understanding the impact of trauma and chronic stress on individuals and communities. We are understanding more deeply how conditions can create negative long-term impacts on physical, mental, and behavioral health. We have learned that we are sometimes unable to fully process the intense feelings that arise when a traumatic event occurs. When this happens, we may repeatedly experience traumatic feelings and perceive threats similar to those we encountered in the original experience. The Pali Canon teaches that karmas "accumulated will not become extinct as long as their results have not been experienced."[52] Mindful awareness is the most direct mode of experience. Under trauma and stress, people often cannot directly experience the emotions and bodily sensations that arise; the sensations are too overwhelming. In extreme cases, people dissociate or have out-of-body experiences.

People who experience intense hunger as children will sometimes develop fraught relationships with food, even after they have plentiful access to it. People who were abused by their parents will often find themselves in relationships where there is abuse. According to karma theory, we don't know when or exactly how a seed planted will fruit. Likewise, the effects of trauma are nonlinear and various. Consider two Jewish siblings I know who lost family members in the Holocaust: one is impoverished and struggles with addiction, the other wealthy and haunted by perfectionism.

Studies show that people with a greater number of adverse childhood experiences—food insecurity, lack of housing, violence, abuse, neglect, and families affected by drug addiction, incarceration, and illness— are more likely to experience an array of mental, behavioral, and physical health problems. These challenges manifest in particular individuals but are collective problems. Oppressive systems like patriarchy and racism create ongoing and intergenerational traumatic conditioning for individuals and entire communities. If we want people to be well, it is essential that we dive into the work of ending adverse conditions for everyone.

In the West, people are awakening to what Buddhists have been saying for thousands of years. What we have experienced, and how we feel about it, has a profound impact on what we experience. We must develop our understanding of how powerful emotions arise and how best to care for each other. Trauma-informed care encourages us to know that conditions matter and know what we can do that will create more beneficial conditions. This verse highlights just how deep these truths are. It is not only trauma and stress that condition our experience, but every single instant of consciousness. We are always planting seeds and seeing their fruit.

It is well-documented that people's individual responses to traumatic events vary widely. When soldiers who had been in the same units and experienced the same close-quarter combat returned to the United States from Vietnam, some of them exhibited serious, lifelong PTSD, while others had only minor challenges. Each soldier's response to combat was also the product of a vast amount of other conditioning. They came to the war with seeds from their childhoods, their families, and the experiences of their ancestors. The whole war, as well as any single personal experience of violence, is inseparable from thousands of years of history. No duality can contain the truth of a single moment of trauma, or of any experience for that matter. We are, as conscious beings, involved in an ongoing process as seeds from the past bear fruit and seeds are planted here in the present. The good news is that we can plant seeds of healing.

When I was healing from PTSD, I practiced seeing that my ideas were not truths, but mere appearances. In Yogacara terms, I was seeing through the grossest level of duality, the dualities made by the thinking mind. I practiced mindfulness of bodily sensations and emotions. I learned new and healthier ways to look at things. I valued my imagination, which allowed me to see my rage as a shackled and tortured wolf and my terror as a cowering child. This helped me bring compassion to parts of myself I habitually ignored or tried to get rid of. Sometimes in meditation I felt a profound peace, while at other times I felt burning rage or warm tears dripping into my hands. As I recall this practice, I have a felt sense that I was seeing "mere appearance," simply noticing what appeared to be arising. I was "directly seeing karma," allowing seeds from the past to bear their fruit as I planted seeds of mindfulness, nonviolence, and compassion.

Often, my feelings were too overwhelming to face. My Zen teacher gently reminded me not to dive in if I could not tolerate my experience. I found ways to soothe and care for myself, such as watching comedies, cultivating stable relationships, attending therapy long-term, sweeping the zendo, and taking baths, deep breaths, breaks during long meditations, and walks where I focused on the birds and the trees. I was healing trauma that was both mine and of countless generations before and after me. I cannot say where the trauma or the healing begin and end.

This verse calls me to turn toward the process of seeing clearly what is here, rather than being caught in my conditioned views of it. Every duality is just a trick of the mind, yet this moment, these words, still appear, as do the distant roar of traffic, aching heart, and overflowing joy. Whether the trauma is yours or mine, in the past or now, surely matters, but it is also just a way of looking at things. We imagine this world where global temperatures rise, where people kill whole families with drones, where millions are imprisoned, where children go hungry while powerful individuals have more personal wealth than millions of other people combined. We are creating this together, and we can create something else. It all arises from the field of mind; we plant the seeds that will flower as the future. Let us keep asking ourselves: What are we planting? We are bound and liberated only within this web of interdependence. May we see through duality, and awaken to the fact that every moment is a chance to heal the world.

30

Thusness and Things

The root consciousness is like the mantra,
Thusness is like the wood,
Conceptualization is like the appearance
Of the elephant, and duality is like the elephant. ||30||

Our habits of thought, feeling, action, and perception entrance and enchant us, mesmerize, hypnotize, and mislead us, but right here and now is the truth. In the last few verses, Vasubandhu invited us to remember that we already know that a conjured illusion of an elephant isn't a real elephant; it is created by our way of seeing. From this we can learn that everything we see comes through our way of seeing. He invited us to trust that we can heal our sense of alienation, our dissatisfaction, and the habits that bind us by knowing that what we think is real is not.

In various texts where Vasubandhu introduces the complete, realized nature he first does it in negative terms: it is the nonexistence of what you think is separate. However, here as in other texts he goes on to speak of the complete, realized nature in its positive aspect. In the simile of the elephant, he now tells us the conjurer has superimposed the illusion of the elephant onto a pile of wood. When you see through the elephant illusion, you see the wood that was present all along. This wood is thusness, tathata, how things actually are. It is the totality of this moment's experience without any part of it being something observed or observing, being here nor there, arising or passing away. Thusness is this moment of experience if you subtract every possible dualistic category or perception: self/other, past/present, present/future, here/there, white/black, quiet/loud. Those dualisms all are illusions arising from mind, so thusness is simply how things are, complete and real.

A carpenter may pour their energy into turning a spindle on a lathe and in that moment have no idea of completing it. You may deeply listen to your mother speak with no thought of judging, fixing, or responding. I have stood in a crowd of clergy outside the door of the Minnesota Pollution Control Agency's offices singing and hearing voices singing, nothing more. You may raise your foot and set it down, and that may be enough, or place your palms together in front of your lips and lean the body forward. I invite you with all my heart to sit still, without making sound, with nothing you are trying to focus on, and nothing you are trying to attain. Practice objectless meditation. The creation of dualities, of a world of objects and alienation, is just a habit of mind, and habits can change. Thusness is already here, but if we pour ourselves into activity with no object, we may come to know it, to trust it. We may come to trust reality.

If you've ever seen a great magic trick, you know how amazing it is to see something that you know cannot possibly be real. This verse says, "Conceptualization is like the appearance of the elephant, and duality is like the elephant." The previous verse says, "The duality is utterly nonexistent, the mere appearance is there." This describes our experience right now. Conceptualization appears, but the dualities it creates aren't real. Yes, it appears that there is a self and there are other things being observed, that there is a present and a past, that there is a ceiling that is separate from the sky, and silence that is separate from honking horns, a me separate from you, and politicians who are horrid and an "I" who is right. Right here in the midst of all of that appearing, we can know that all the dualities are illusions. You can use your mind and your concepts to be mindful of this. You can practice meditation and wholehearted activity to know it ever more deeply as what is right here. It is not some fearsome elephant, but a pile of sticks: It is simple, no big deal, complete realization, just this, thusness.

31

Knowledge, Relinquishment, and Realization

In understanding how things really are,
The three characteristics are employed together
Corresponding respectively with knowing,
Relinquishment, and attainment. ||31||

When we see how things really are, nothing is destroyed or left out. Everything is included. The complete, realized nature is thusness, reality, but only in relationship with the imaginary and dependent natures. This is not about escape from our imaginations or the vast web of our dependent sufferings—it's about going for refuge within it. True understanding is an integration. Generally speaking, human beings take the imaginary nature of things to be real. With practice we can learn to see how it is constructed by our habits of mind. We can learn to be aware of the dependent nature of each and all things, and we can practice and let go of it all and rest in the complete, realized nature: thusness, or the ungraspability, and incomprehensibility of the moment. As we deepen our awareness of these three natures, we can begin to think about and directly perceive that they are all present in every moment. This is how we can understand how things really are.

In the second half of this verse, Vasubandhu ties the three natures to the first discourse of the Buddha. There he taught the Four Noble Truths: suffering, the cause of suffering, the end of suffering, and the path to end suffering. This seminal sutra first defines and introduces these four truths, then it states that suffering should be *known*, the cause should be *relinquished*, the end should be *attained*, and the path should be *developed*. Buddha says that the proof of his awakening is that he has known, relinquished, attained, and developed each one, respectively. Vasubandhu here says that the imaginary nature should be known, the dependent relinquished, and the complete, realized attained. The three natures correspond to the first three noble truths.

To see things as they really are, we must know the imaginary nature of things and all its attendant sufferings. We must relinquish the dependent nature, letting go of what appears to come and go. We must attain the complete, realized nature, see the emptiness of all that appears solid, and rest in thusness.

Recall that in verse 5 Vasubandhu says that the imaginary nature is mind, and then goes on to explain that mind is alaya, manas, and the six senses. Understanding our mind is knowing the imaginary nature.

To know the imaginary nature is to know suffering and not to turn away. Cornel West once wrote, "You must let suffering speak if you want to hear the truth." The first discourse defines suffering, dukkha, as birth, aging, illness, death, separation from things liked, association with things liked, and not getting what one wants. This teaching does not deny the joys of childbirth, the wisdom of aging, or the moments of profound intimacy that come with death. But we are called here to know and to care about anguish. Speaking of the moment when a child's head emerges from its mother's vagina, the artist Judy Chicago once wrote, "If men had babies there would be thousands of images of the crowning." Too many of us miss the truth of the courage, physical pain, and countless lives lost in childbirth. Let us know birth more completely. Let us not turn away, either, from death. Let us not ignore or furtively whisper death, but speak it, know it together. We are called to know the pain of hunger, the rage of millions imprisoned, the shame of being ignored, held back, and erased, and the pain of knowing that your wealth, safety, and success arrives in part on the backs of people held down by vast systems of harm. We cannot heal if we do not acknowledge these truths. Recall though that this text says that knowing the truth of suffering is knowing the imaginary nature. All of this is dependent on how we view it. Our personal and collective habits of mind, emotion, and action produce this imagination, this suffering. It's not ultimately real, and it is not fixed. We are engaged in transformation. What can we imagine together if we really choose to know suffering?

The second noble truth, the cause of suffering, is "the craving that makes for further becoming."[53] The first teaching says that this cause of suffering can be relinquished, and Vasubandhu says this corresponds to the dependent nature. We can let go of wanting things to be other than how they are, even as we devote our lives to the alleviation of suffering. In earlier verses, Vasubandhu points out that the dependent nature is what appears. In this moment due to infinite conditions something appears. He goes on to say that the problem is that we try to grasp it. We can learn to relinquish craving, and we can learn to not try to grasp things within this vast web of interdependence. Our life can be one of offering and letting go. A life of giving is available to you.

The third noble truth is the end of suffering, "the remainderless fading and cessation, renunciation, relinquishment, release, and letting go of that very craving." The first teaching says this third noble truth should be attained, and this verse says that seeing the complete, realized nature is this very attainment, this ending, this letting go. When the mind is not grasping things as objects, there is nothing to grasp, to desire, to avoid, or to misunderstand.

To see clearly we can bring these views together: knowing suffering, relinquishing desire for things which are mere interdependence, and attaining freedom from the suffering of want. These are the first three noble truths, and the fourth is the eightfold path: holistic view, intention, speech, action, livelihood, effort, mindfulness, and meditation. In short, cultivate a wise intention to alleviate suffering, act with compassion, and learn to heal the mind.

32

Both Perception and Nonperception

It is said that knowledge is nonperception,
Relinquishment is nonappearance,
Groundless perception, though,
Is attainment, direct realization. ||32||

When we fully know the first noble truth of suffering, we perceive no object. There is no gap between ourselves and suffering, or what is seen. As we relinquish craving, the view of the world that comes from our habits of mind does not appear. When we attain the third noble truth, the end of suffering, there is perception that does not arise from karma, there is only reality. In the Pali Canon one of the highest states of meditative experience, *jhanas*, is called "neither perception, nor nonperception." Here Vasubandhu offers perception *and* nonperception as the ultimate state.

The term *anupalambha*, nonperception, is used in various technical ways in ancient Indian literature. It sometimes refers to a type of intuitive knowledge that is beyond ordinary cognition. It might be translated as without conception or projection. Toward the end of Vasubandhu's "Thirty Verses," he refers to attainment as "when consciousness does not perceive any object." This does not refer to blankness, but to the absence of the aspect of mind that makes it seem like there is a subject viewing objects. This aspect, you may recall, is called *manas* in the eight-consciousness model.

The knowledge that marks liberation from suffering is the knowing of suffering, which is the imaginary nature, and this knowing is nondual awareness. It is experience where no subject or object appears. Mahayana texts emphasize the deep relationship between compassion and emptiness. This verse holds forth the possibility that we can be completely liberated from suffering by realizing that we are inseparable from it. It may help to think of compassion as more of a space than a feeling. We can develop this capacity with objectless meditation or cultivating panoramic awareness, which includes every aspect of experience: sights, sounds, smells, tastes, body, and mind, without preference. It is possible to be a healing space for someone who is overwhelmed: You can be with their tears, silences, or shouting, or sit with people who are holding it all in, or hold space in our hearts for those who have caused terrible harm. It is possible for our bodies to move in a way that cares for our communities as easily as a hand reaches to adjust a pillow in the night.

Please know this capacity is available, but know that it is not to be expected. Usually our compassion is marked by a sense of duality and false perceptions, and by our own complex, conditioned reactivities. We can become exhausted and overwhelmed as we practice healing our hearts, our loved ones, and our planet. Let us practice and develop mindfulness of body and emotions, so that we may care for whatever arises in ourselves. There is grave danger in deluding ourselves that we have attained the ability to perfectly manifest compassion with no gap. We may become prideful, or pitying, or even simply burn out if we ignore our real experience based on this ideal. Please make time to care for and cultivate healthy boundaries even as you open to boundlessness.

The relinquishment of craving that marks the end of suffering is the nonappearance of karmically conditioned views. The image of a world of things to get or get rid of does not appear. It is merely a habit of mind that the world is like this, and habits can change. In the Pali Canon we find this passage: "There is, monks, an unborn, unbecome, unmade, unconditioned. If, monks, there was no unborn, unbecome, unmade, unconditioned, no escape would be discerned from what is born, become, made, conditioned."[54] Generally, Early Buddhist texts uphold the value and possibility of escape from suffering. Mahayana literature emphasizes liberation within suffering.

Regardless, they have deep and common themes. Here the point is to realize that the world is already not what our habits of mind make it to be. We can experience this directly, but it can help to remember it.

Megan Phelps Roper was raised in the Westboro Baptist Church, which is most famous for protesting the funerals of gay military service members with signs declaring hatred toward LGBTQ folks. She participated fully and knew for certain that God would send gay people to eternal hell. As she met and made friends with folks via social media, she came to believe that her own views—and those of her church—were wrong, and she left. The process was apparently very painful, but she is now out in the world, writing books and giving interviews, showing how we can become free of our views. We need help to be humble. There are people alive today, and people wiser than me in the past and the future, who would see my viewpoints as ridiculous, harmful, and benighted. I try to recall that only habits of mind make things appear to me as they do, and that right here and now there is something beyond my conditioned view. This helps me to relinquish both my own suffering and habits that cause harm.

Attainment of liberation from suffering is groundless perception. There is nothing to hold onto, nothing to let go of, or to get rid of. There is no you or me or I. No inside, outside, or in between. There is perception, but not perception of something. A classic Zen story illustrates this:

> Zhaozhou asked Nanquan, "What is the Way?"
>
> Nanquan answered, "Ordinary mind is the Way."
>
> Zhaozhou asked, "Should I turn toward it or not?"
>
> Nanquan said, "If you turn toward it, you turn away from it."
>
> Zhaozhou asked, "How can I know the Way if I don't turn toward it?"
>
> Nanquan answered, "The Way is not about knowing or not knowing. When you know something you are deluded, and when you don't know, you are just empty-headed. When you reach the Way beyond doubt, it is as vast as infinite space. You can't say it's right or wrong." With these words Zhaozhou had sudden understanding.[55]

Practicing objectlessness opens space for awakening to how things already are. Ordinary mind is already the totality of experience. It is the whole of what is known. For me right now, there is the ringing in my ears, the light reflecting on my wooden wedding ring, the chair and my body, these words, a gray sky outside an icy window, and so much more. We can pour ourselves into life with our whole hearts: reading, typing, measuring tea, planning a project. If you want to realize objectlessness, practicing with simple things will help. Just sitting in an upright posture, bowing, walking slowly, or turning a key in a lock are wondrous ways to practice ordinary mind.

33

Let It All Go

Through not perceiving duality,
The dual form vanishes.
Through vanishing, the realized,
Nonduality, is attained. ||33||

The world looks very different when duality disappears, and it does not. When William James researched religious experiences from around the world, he found a consistent theme: ineffability. People said that their deep spiritual experiences were beyond words, and yet they spoke. Our experience right now is surely beyond words. How could you completely describe the whole of your field of experience in this moment—all of the sights, sounds, smells, tastes, bodily sensations, thoughts and feelings? Though a few words might point the way, a lifetime of writing would not fully capture it. The dualities inherent in language are wondrous, and they are incomplete. In retreat at our Zen center we uphold the ancient way of taking time to commit to not speaking, to pouring ourselves into the silence as well as the sounds of passing traffic sounds or the rise and fall of the breath. We give the mind space to soften and release from the dualisms of language. We make space for attaining nonduality. Ultimately, we might find that words, too, are not other than the whole. Nothing is ever left out of the completeness of the nonduality that is already here.

> One day during her morning sitting [the laywoman Asan] heard the crow of the rooster, and her mind suddenly opened. She spoke a verse in response:

> > The fields, the mountains, the flowers, and my body too are the voice of the bird—what is left that can be said to hear?[56]

Everything is fully flowering in nonduality. In Vasubandhu's "Thirty Verses," he says that in experiences like this, the manas is not found. In other Yogacara literature, they say this describes the state where the manas consciousness is transformed into the wisdom of equality as the alaya is transformed into the great mirror wisdom. Consciousness can fully show reality as it is with equanimity. There is often a wild and simple joy that arrives with this kind of experience. The Chan nun Zhenru wrote:

I suddenly find myself upside down on level
   ground
When I pick myself up I find there's nothing to say
If someone should ask me what this is all about,
Smiling, I'd point to the pure breeze and the bright
   moon.[57]

It's beyond words; she is irrepressible. This section of the "Treatise on Three Natures" points toward a radical transformation which happens, and which can happen with you. My teacher recalls Shunryu Suzuki saying, "Enlightenment is an accident, and zazen makes you accident-prone." I think though, that it's helpful to notice that our opening to nonduality can be partial and gradual.

A friend who was living in a halfway house for recovering addicts was consumed with resentment toward their inconsiderate and bullying housemate. They fought. There was shouting. My friend made space between their bed and their dresser to practice meditation and attune to their feelings and their body. They turned toward the anger, the burning sensations in their chest, and their clenching hands. They began to feel more intimacy with themselves and the sounds of the household, the texture of the carpet, the play of light. They turned their thoughts toward the suffering of their housemate, and they began to feel more con-nection and less alienation. They found some clarity about their own needs and began to learn how to be assertive and how to let go of trying to control. Hardened dualities softened, and a little space in the relationship opened. The household environment was still challenging, but much less so. Since then, this old friend has spent years in recovery, and also in addiction, rehab, and halfway homes. They suffer, they heal, and I believe that their practice matters every day.

In Zen literature, we often use the word *intimacy* to point to nonduality. Everything is already intimate, and we can learn to know this intimacy. When we recognize this inherent intimacy we tend to feel connected, supported, and engaged. When we are far from seeing it, we feel cut off, unsupported, and become focused on controlling things. I encourage you to notice where you feel this kind of intimacy and to turn toward it, to take time to let it in. When you feel nonintimate, find ways to open to the connection to all of life that is already there. You can feel your way toward awakening, and find the joy, the peace, and the power there. You may also suddenly realize there is no I to wake up and nothing to wake up to, only awakeness itself.

34

Seeing Through the Magic Trick

Just like with the illusion,
The nonperception of the elephant,
The vanishing of its form, and the perception
Of the piece of wood all occur at once. ||34||

When I was a child, I had a book of optical illusions. I can recall measuring two lines on the paper with my wooden ruler and seeing that the ruler said they were equal in length. I could see for certain, just by looking, that one was longer. With another page I would gaze at the image of a flock of birds, and suddenly instead I saw two faces. I'd look up and around the room with a fresh sense of the magic of being alive. Scientists interested in the way humans construct experience often focus on the perceptual processes that create these kinds of optical experiences. This verse compares the experience of awakening to that moment when our view of an illusion flips, suddenly and completely.

Here Vasubandhu says that there is a sudden moment of realization where we don't see the elephant, we don't see the image that we thought was an elephant, and we see what is actually there: a pile of sticks. The elephant is the imaginary nature, the image that we take to be an elephant is the dependent nature, and the wood is the complete, realized nature. We aren't faced with a huge imposing thing we believe we must contend with, which doesn't actually exist. We haven't turned the dependent flux of reality into what we believe is a thing, separate from other things. We are at rest in experience where no duality appears; there is not an I viewing things, nor things in relation to other things. There is—for lack of a better way to put it—just this.

Verse 30 says, "The root consciousness is like the mantra, / Thusness is like the wood." Alaya is the mantra that creates the illusion of the elephant, thusness is what is actually here. It is the habits of consciousness that create the illusion. We have vast accumulations of seeds in the storehouse: seeds of wanting, compassion, fear, envy, irritation, kindness, shame, energy, exhaustion, and so much more. We have seeds that form our image and experience of our own bodies, and of colors, sounds, flavors, or letters on a page. Let us marvel that in this moment so that many seeds come to fruition so these words can emerge on the page and you can understand them. Each letter and each tiny motion of a knuckle on a finger is the result of vast amounts of conditioning, or karma. Because the mantra causes the illusion, we can plant seeds for the alaya to be transformed so we can see what is here: not a world of alienation, but reality, interdependent and complete. Here there is nothing to be gained or avoided, merely the energy of life flowing to manifest freedom and wellness.

In the Mahamudra text *The Bright Torch*, the yogin Tsele Natsok Rangdrol quotes one of the greatest yoginis of the Tibetan tradition, Niguma:

> The only thing that matters is recognizing the true nature, the true meaning of the mind exactly as it is, and to know how to maintain the natural state of the ordinary mind, just as it happens to be, without polluting it with mental fabrication. According to Jnana-dakini Niguma:

> > If you do not know that whatever appears
> > is meditation
> > how can you attain it through relying on
> > remedies?
> > You cannot eliminate objects and conditions by eliminating them,
> > but if you know they are illusions, they
> > are spontaneously liberated.[58]

Planting beneficial seeds does not mean fixing or judging. The mind of meditation is a mind that does not try to destroy or control. It is a mind of nonviolence, where nothing is excluded. When we practice nonviolence, we plant seeds of not seeing a world of things to be dominated. When we practice generosity, we plant seeds of not seeing a world of things to be kept or acquired. When we deeply listen to others' sufferings, we plant seeds for a world that is not ignored. When we become ever more mindful of our feelings, we attune to the current natural state of mind, without controlling or ignoring. When we practice objectless meditation, we put down remedies—our efforts to fix, gain, or control—and rest in what is. My dear friend Shodo Spring, a lifelong ecological activist, once said, "We need to wake up to the fact that we don't have to fix nature."

We can see through illusion, and we can do it together. When my grandmother was born, women couldn't vote in the United States. When I was born, women generally couldn't get credit cards in their own names. The pandemic of sexual violence was largely hidden, unspoken. In 2020, activists helped me wake up to the ongoing violence and hatred directed toward Asian people in my home nation. The knowing that characterizes the awakening Vasubandhu is talking about is the knowing of the first noble truth, the truth of suffering. The sudden awakening Vasubandhu offers as possible is sudden but inseparable from the practice of seeing through delusion. The bliss and freedom are real, and they are not apart from suffering or samsara. They are of dependent nature.

35

Projection Only

By these reasons—minds cause contrary views,
Minds see unreal things,
Accordance with the three knowledges, and
Effortless attainment of liberation— ||35||

Here Vasubandhu refers to four Yogacara proofs, found in the *Mahayanasamgraha*, for the claim that we don't experience anything apart from the constructions of mind.[59] This central principle of Yogacara thought is called *vijnaptimatra*. Some common translations are "projection only," "conception only," "mere concept," or "mere representation." At the climax of Vasubandhu's "Thirty Verses on Consciousness Only," he says that liberation is when consciousness rests in vijnaptimatra. This occurs when consciousness abides in the apparent moment without the sense that there is a subject viewing objects. The *Mahayanasamgraha* teaches that when we truly understand the three natures, we realize projection only. When you become overwhelmed, remember that it's okay, for it's only projection. When you become complacent, remember that it's projection only, and that you are contributing to what will be projected.

The first proof states that "minds cause contrary views." Just follow politics in the newspapers and it will be pretty evident that contrary views exist. Regardless of what we think, we think it because of mental processes. Looking at what we might say is a large piece of poster board with a picture and black marks on it, one person may see a poster with an amazing piece of literature inscribed, another the basis for a brutal colonialist way of thinking, another (perhaps a dog) something to chew on, and another (perhaps a baby) an insurmountable wall.

Generally Yogacara texts explain this proof by referring to people in the various Buddhist realms of existence: the hell, hungry ghost, animal, human, fighting spirit, and god realms. Early Buddhist teachings say that people are reborn in these various realms based on their karma until they attain nirvana, at which point the cycle stops. Many Buddhists believe that these realms and rebirth are real. Modernist Buddhists often like to say they are merely psychological states. Yogacarins say we see these realms and what are in them based on our mental habits (our karma). Yogacara teachings are an early doctrinal basis clearly supporting the modernist view as well as the traditional view. They support both, saying that what we think is real, the realm we're in, is always projection only.

Dogen Zenji refers to this proof in his *Mountains and Waters Sutra*. Here he uses water as a metaphor for thusness:

> Some beings see water as wondrous blossoms . . . Hungry ghosts see water as a raging fire or pus and blood. Dragons see water as a palace or a pavilion. Some beings see water as the seven treasures or a wish-granting jewel. Some beings see water as a forest or a wall. Some see it as the Dharma nature of pure liberation, the true human body, or as the form of body and essence of mind. Human beings see water as water. Water is seen as dead or alive depending on causes and conditions.[60]

I was raised with a materialist, scientific mindset. I was taught that water is not alive. It is hydrogen and oxygen. Lately though, I have begun to follow the leadership of Indigenous water protectors who base their ecological activism on their knowledge that water is alive. Water is a living part of this world that needs protection and care. These are all just ways of seeing, and it is within them and in relationship to it all that I can look for a way to act for the well-being of the world.

The second proof is that we see things that aren't real. We have dreams where we feel, see, hear, smell, and taste. We can hear sounds or see things that are not physically present when we remember or imagine. We can hallucinate. We know that mind can make a total simulacrum of what we think is a real experience, and for this reason we can't ultimately know that this moment of experience right now is not purely made by mind. You have woken from a dream a thousand times. There is no way to know that you won't wake from this life and realize it was a dream, or forget it as you have forgotten so many other dreams.

The third proof refers to three types of mental attainment or knowledges of great meditators from the Mahayana, Theravada, and Yogacara traditions. First, some bodhisattvas can imagine and be in whatever realm they choose. Their mental control is so great that they can create whatever experience they want: floating through space on a cloud, holding hands with a dead friend, sitting at the feet of a great teacher. On one hand, this seems outside my experience. However, many years ago I often found myself lucid dreaming, and I could choose to fly and visit beautiful landscapes at will. I did this with no training. The experience was real and powerful. Tibetan Buddhists train the mind to develop amazing capacities of imagination, creating vivid and complete sensory experiences. There is no way to know the limits of this capacity for imagination. The second type of knowledge this verse refers to is that of great practitioners of

Early Buddhism, *arhats*. They learned to bring the dharmas into view. Rather than seeing the apparent solid reality we live in, they see the flickering coming into being and passing away of thousands of dharmas in each moment: color, shape, feeling, loudness, pressure, and more. Third, people can realize the nondual awareness upheld by this text and see that there are not ultimately real things, unless they are made by the processes of mind into things. The Mahayana, Theravada, and Yogacara teachings all revere people who attain a way of knowing that affirms what the *Dhammapada* says in its opening line, "Our life is shaped by our mind."[61]

The last of the four proofs in this verse is the opposite of what it appears to be. The fact that effortless liberation is *not* possible is a proof for projection only. The meaning of this reference is evident only from reading the more-lengthy proof this verse refers to in the *Mahayanasamgraha*. I'm sorry if you were hoping for some effortless liberation. It is possible that Vasubandhu is subtly taking a nondual position on the matter: effortless liberation is both absurd and possible, but this is an unpopular interpretation. Recall the basic Buddhist idea that nirvana, liberation from suffering, is seeing clearly. It is seeing dharmata, realness. This proof states that if we weren't seeing projections only (vijnaptimatra), we would already be seeing reality, which means we'd be effortlessly free from suffering. People suffer, this is quite evident. People also heal, but I haven't seen liberation without effort. Even when freedom comes from letting go, we still have to open our hands, and sometimes that is hard. Seeing clearly takes effort. Even surrender comes through struggle.

We suffer together and alone in so many ways: we experience fear, anger, and shame. We hunger for a dinner that will not come, feel the anger of a woman who has to question whether it's safe to walk home after a party, sense the clenched hands of young immigrants at the sight of police lights, the sorrow of a nonbinary person faced with two options, men's and women's. Families grieve loved ones killed by American-made drones. The last nesting pair of a species of birds that has lived for a million years struggle and fail to raise chicks in a hot and furious hurricane year. It's not all the same, but it all matters, and liberation is not free. Exactly at the culmination of his proof that we know only projection, Vasubandhu reminds us to practice, to offer our energy to liberation, and to lead a life conducive to freedom from suffering.

36

There Is No Mind in Mind-Only

Through the perception of mind-only,
There is no perception of knowable things.
Through the nonperception of knowable things,
There is no perception of mind. ||36||

When we realize that we don't have an experience outside of the one mediated by mind, we realize that we don't perceive any actual things. When we don't see actual things, we realize we don't have a mind that grasps them, for the mind that grasps is dependent on things to grasp. We can realize that things and mind are empty. Empty simply means they have no separate, lasting nature. The previous verse presented four cognitive proofs for vijnaptimatra, projection only, which in this verse Vasubandhu calls cittamatra, mind-only. Sometimes he suggests we use the mind's discriminating abilities to help us get free of them. In this verse we are invited into a more meditative approach. In the commentary on verse 24, I offered these similar lines from the *Mahayanasamgraha*:

Bodhisattvas in meditative equipoise
See that images are mind—
Through putting an end to the notions of
    referents,
They determine them as their very own notions.

Thus, the mind dwells on the inside.
They realize that the apprehended does not exist,
Thereby realizing that there is no apprehender
    [either].
Therefore, they are in touch with the
    unobservable.[62]

We can come to touch the truth that is right here. There are not really things observed and something observing; those divisions are merely mind appearing to create an illusion of mind and things. Yogacara teachings offer two principal methods for arriving at this realization: vipassana and samatha. The meditative analysis of vipassana, or insight, helps us cut through the habits of mind that make the things we are perceiving seem separate from the process of perception. Samatha, objectless meditation, plants the seeds of putting down all conceptualization and objectification so we realize what is already here: the complete, realized nature, no things, no mind.

This verse makes clear that in Vasubandhu's Yogacara, the terms "mind only" and "projection only" do not refer to a solipsistic state where we dwell in total subjectivity. They do not refer to the realization of a transcendent mental self. They don't intend to prove or argue that everything is made of consciousness. There is no mind in mind-only. Nonduality reigns here. The problem is that we get caught up in our perception that there are absolutely real things and that we are truly separate from them. This perception binds us to the cycle of things to grasp and things to push away, to all the anguish and harm that follows, and to life and death. A radical freedom from all these is available.

The great sixteenth-century Zen nun Soshin wrote of mind-only using a term often found in Zen and Mahamudra texts: "original mind." We sometimes see this translated as "ordinary mind" or "straightforward mind." She offered these teachings for challenging times; in *Zen Women,* Grace Schireson described her as "a woman teaching other women, some of whom are trapped as sexual slaves, and all of them being in a fiercely political and emotional hotbed of power, intrigue, and seduction." Soshin wrote:

> If you are continuously aware of the con-
> stancy of no-thing-ness, that things have
> no self-function, you will be following the
> original mind. One moves beyond, one tran-
> scends grasping pleasure and averting from

> suffering to see and follow the original mind.
> This is finding ease in [the midst of] every-
> day life; this is true joy. Therefore, you don't
> have to go away to the mountain, it is within
> your own mind.[63]

There is something wonderful available to you, your original mind, a mind that doesn't see objects. Soshin's teaching reflects the words of the first half of this verse of our text, "Through the perception of mind only, there is no perception of knowable things." She brings forth the central message of Buddhism: you can realize nonsuffering. Joy is possible wherever we are. It is not somewhere else outside of this moment of experience, of original mind. Teachings on original mind can help point the way but can sound a bit like they claim that mind is a lasting transcendental real- ity. Like the second half of this verse, Zen teachers offer antidotes like this line from master Hongzhi: "Embodying and fulfilling the way of nonmind, finally you can rest." The precise philosophical articulation of nondualism Vasubandhu uses can be overwhelm- ing. It can be hard to look at both sides now. Some- times it may help us to emphasize, as Soshin does, one side with teachings on original mind.

Tibetan teachings often say mind is both luminous and empty. They affirm mind as something that reveals or illuminates an apparent world, and also invite us to see that it has no separate, lasting nature. Thus mind and no-mind are harmonized. The *Diamond Sutra* plays with this nonduality:

> "Subhuti, what do you think? Suppose there were as many Ganges Rivers as there are sands in the Ganges. And suppose there were as many buddha worlds as there are sands in all these Ganges Rivers. Would they be many or would they not?"
>
> "They would be very many, World-Honored One." The Buddha then said to Subhuti, "The different types of minds possessed by the living beings in these various lands—the Thus Come One knows them all. Why? Because the Thus Come One teaches that these various types of minds are all of them not minds. So they are called minds. Why do I say this? Subhuti, past mind cannot be gotten hold of, present mind cannot be gotten hold of, future mind cannot be gotten hold of."[64]

On Earth, we conscious beings are various, and we hold so many different opinions, conditions, feelings, and ways of seeing. The Buddha says he knows them all in this way: their experience can't be grasped. We will not be able to hold onto mind then, now, or someday. We are all different, and we share the condition of being here in flux of reality. We share the fact that we can't ultimately grasp or hold onto anything. All that comes to be eventually passes away. These teachings promise that we all share the capacity to rest, and to find joy and a compassionate way of living within this process by realizing that there are not things and we are not separate from them.

37

Enter Where You Are

Through not perceiving either,
The Dharma realm is perceived
Through perceiving the Dharma realm,
Unlimitedness is perceived. ||37||

Recently I heard a talk by a Dakota elder named Bob Klanderud. He spoke of the total kinship of all life. He told us that the confluence of the Mississippi and Minnesota rivers, near my home on U.S.–occupied Dakota land, is called Bdote. For the Dakota, Bdote is the origin of the universe, the land of genesis. In his words, "It is Eden." He asked us, "Now that you know you live in Eden, how will you choose to live?"

The previous verse taught us that first we see that there are not things, and then we see that there is no mind. This verse speaks of not seeing things or mind, and thus seeing the Dharma realm—reality as liberation and well-being—and thus seeing infinite possibility without limitations. In the "Thirty Verses," Vasubandhu says, when the dependent nature is not seen, the complete, realized nature is not seen. All this is possible because of mutual dependence.

Dharmadhatu, or Dharma realm, means everything that is perceived. As we've already discussed, *Dharma* with a capital "D" means "truth," "reality," and "correct teaching"; *dharma* with a lowercase "d" means "phenomena." *Dhatu* means "realm" or "element." Here all these meanings are collapsed. The totality of your experience, your realm, is reality. Every particular phenomena has the reality element, dharmadhatu. What is dharmadhatu? It is that nothing is what you imagine it to be. It is not mind, it is not things. It is of dependent nature. It is unlimited. Nothing can bind it, because it has no edges, no thingness. It is infinite possibility and total freedom. Not freedom from dependence, but the freedom of total interdependence.

Shitou's "Song of the Grass Roof Hermitage" tells of profound ease and deep engagement with simple living. Shitou writes, "Though the hut is small it includes the entire world." "Entire world" is a translation of dharmadhatu. Everything is included in Shitou's chosen life of poverty in a tiny mountain hut. If we want to realize unlimitedness, it helps to take time to retire into small and quiet quarters, to settle into retreat. My mind is filled right now with the radiant face of my dear Vietnamese friend Venerable Thuan Bach. She spent three years in rigorous solo retreat and now manifests such joyfulness and energy for her community! We may not choose that degree of commitment, but I pray we may find the time for daily meditation, for simple work, for taking days, or maybe weeks or months to devote ourselves to slowing down and really seeing what's here. This is not about escaping from reality. It is about escaping to reality.

Dharmadhatu is a central theme in the *Avatamsaka Sutra*, and the Huayan school of Buddhism that emerged shortly after Yogacara. That body of teaching emphasizes interdependence, social engagement, diversity, skillful means, and mind-blowing imagery. The teachers in the *Avatamsaka* are girls, boys, queens, nuns, monks, goddesses, great bodhisattvas, mendicants, and laborers. They use countless practices: words, music, physical touch, food offerings, perfumes, miracles, mathematics, grammar, and more. Again and again, they show that it's all connected, it's all particular, and it's all amazing. How will we act if we realize we are in the Dharma realm?

The word *dhatu* has powerful associations in Buddhist texts. Some of the earliest records of Buddhist practice describe worshiping a piece of the Buddha's body entombed in a monument called a stupa. The piece of the body—a finger bone for example—was called the *buddha dhatu*, the Buddha element. Buddhists walk meditatively and worshipfully around these stupas. In the Pali Canon, the Buddha teaches, "One who sees the Dhamma, sees me."[65] Teachings of the all-pervading dharmadhatu invite us into reverential engagement with each particular, and the whole of our experience, not just stupas. These stupas were also known as *dhatu garbha*, the element womb. Around the time that Yogacara teachings arise we also begin to see teachings on the *tathagatha garbha*, the Buddha womb. Tathagata garbha is often translated as "Buddha nature." It is the Buddha element which is inherent in everyone. We are invited into reverence for ourselves and every person as infused with the element of Buddhahood.

Here is a classic Chinese poem attributed to "Plum Blossom Nun":

> The entire day I searched for spring, but spring I
> could not find,
> In my straw sandals I tramped among the moun-
> tain peak clouds.
> Home again, smiling, I finger a sprig of fragrant
> plum blossom;
> Spring was right here on these branches in all of its
> glory![66]

Reality is, by definition, how things already are. The complete, realized nature can't be somewhere else. We already are not things or mind. It just seems that way. We already are not bound by limitations. It just seems that way. We are not separate from the bliss, liberation, and compassion that buddhas represent; we are not separate from the Dharma realm. It just seems that way. We seem to live, though, within this seeming. We suffer and cause harm, and we can heal. So let us choose to tramp the path, to walk, to look, to smell, to taste, to listen, to speak, to care for the mind and heart and whatever floats through them, and to pour ourselves into relationship with our communities. We are inseparable from the healing and liberation of awakening, and so I encourage you—and I vow to join you—on this path of healing and liberation.

38

This Very Body, for Everyone

Through perceiving unlimitedness,
Accomplishing well-being for self and others,
The wise know unsurpassable awakening,
The threefold body. ||38||

I invite you to feel the motion of the belly as the body breathes. Feel your contact with the ground. Feel the sensations in the face. Notice the sensations of the whole body. This text invites us home to where we are embodied. We arrive at the first foundation of mindfulness—the body. I pray that we may ever deepen our awareness and our sensitivity to the body. May we sense our fingertips on the fur of a cat, a damp breeze on a bitter day, soapy hands on a rough-hewn cup, the pain in our neck, our burning eyes, tears on our cheeks, and the ache of a face that has smiled for hours.

The three bodies of buddha are an innovation of the Yogacara that we see reflected throughout Mahayana and Vajrayana Buddhism. *Nirmanakaya* is the manifestation body. It is the physical, temporal body of an incarnate buddha. Siddhartha Gautama, for example, was a nirmanakaya. *Samboghakaya* is the bliss body. This is the body of a bodhisattva that is characterized by blissful feelings and the ability to bring bliss to others. When someone really understands the imaginary nature, they can choose to live in a world of things, of apparent selves, this world of conflict and loss, and experience it as bliss. They can exist within interdependence without being caught by the idea that there are things to control. By being joyful, they help others realize this joy. *Dharmakaya* is the Dharma body. It is the complete, realized nature of the body, which means it has no self nature. It is empty of separation and duration. Thus the dharmakaya can't, by definition, be separate from anything, so it is always everywhere. This is why your body is the buddha, and your body is the universe, and your body is not a thing. It is not an object to be held or controlled.

In the *Rohitassa Sutta* of the Pali Canon, the Buddha says, "It is just within this fathom-long body, with its perception & intellect, that I declare that there is the cosmos, the origination of the cosmos, the cessation of the cosmos, and the path of practice leading to the cessation of the cosmos."[67]

The *Ultimate Supreme Path of the Mahamudra* states,

The entire array of thought and nonthought,
appearances and no-appearance, resting and no
    resting,
empty and not empty, clarity and no clarity,
all are one taste in the luminosity of the
    dharmakaya."[68]

This verse says when we realize unlimitedness, we know these three bodies. We realize we are buddha, we awaken to the bliss of being here in this troubled world, and we realize this body is the universe and the universe is this body. Thus we will want to take care of things. To realize unlimitedness is to see infinite possibility. Once we have landed on an exact vision of what is possible, we have lost what Katagiri Roshi called our "dim vision." We are invited here into a fertile darkness. Sometimes, it is the very hiddenness of the path enshrouded in drifting mists that awakens us to our walking. Most of the time I've spent with my teacher, Tim Burkett, has been in the stillness of zazen in the dim light just before the dawn.

I have been called an idealist because of my work to dismantle racism, patriarchy, and the objectification of the Earth, but honestly, I have no idea what the outcome of the work will be. My practice is to show up, to listen, to speak up, and to try to do it with compassion and an open mind. I don't know whether we'll have even more massive climate catastrophes in the future, or if we'll find some way to change course. I don't know whether our future will look like *The Handmaid's Tale* or ever-growing liberation. I do believe that the possibilities are limitless and that this moment is limitlessly connected to it all, and that what I do matters.

This final verse of Vasubandhu's work mirrors the language of the *Heart Sutra,* which speaks of unsurpassable awakening, *anuttaram bodhi.* It also mirrors the language of the four vows with which we end Zen services:

> Being are numberless, vowing to free them
> Delusions are inexhaustible, vowing to end them
> Dharma gates are boundless, vowing to enter them
> Buddha's Way is unsurpassable, vowing to become it.

You cannot go beyond what is already unlimited. All this freedom is to be accomplished for self and others. All this nonduality is for us to manifest caring for our own frail, heartbroken selves, and for everyone and everything. This is about accomplishing well-being, engaging in the activity of healing the particular selves and others we meet. We can realize this unlimitedness in listening with our whole hearts, in being honest with others when we feel wronged, in sending money to a community organization, in tending with dirty hands to a green friend living in the dark loam of the garden. The great civil rights activist Fannie Lou Hamer said, "Nobody's free until everybody's free." She saw our interdependence and our limitless possibility. She also said, "If I fall, I'll fall five feet four inches forward in the fight for freedom." Her way of "fighting" was to meet violence with disciplined nonviolence. Within her fathom-long body she realized, through action, new possibilities of liberation.

The three bodies of buddha are here. Our body is of three natures. We can feel, right now, the sensations of the body in its momentary manifestation. We imagine it to be like this, separate and lasting, but it is merely an apparent manifestation of infinite dependencies. We can experience this and find the bliss of being free of our ideas about it. It is already empty of separation, duration, and not bound by our thinking. We are the whole, the universe; we are complete and real. If it does not seem this way to you, that's okay. Meditation and ethical living open the way to realization. The promise of this text is that freedom is available. We can embody it together with open hands, warm smiles, and bliss in the midst of our aching awakening hearts.

Trisvabhāvanirdeśaḥ

त्रिस्वभावनिर्देशः

कल्पितः परतन्त्रश्च परिनिष्पन्न एव च ।
त्रयः स्वभावा धीराणां गम्भीरज्ञेयमिष्यते ॥१ ॥
kalpitaḥ paratantraś ca pariniṣpanna eva ca|
trayaḥ svabhāvā dhīrāṇāṃ gambhīrajñeyam iṣyate ||1||

यत् ख्याति परतन्त्रोऽसौ यथा ख्याति स कल्पितः ।
प्रत्ययाधीनवृत्तित्वात् कल्पनामात्रभावतः ॥२ ॥
yat khyāti paratantro'sau yathā khyāti sa kalpitaḥ|
pratyayādhīnavṛttitvāt kalpanāmātrabhāvataḥ ||2||

तस्य ख्यातुर्यथाख्यानं या सदाविद्यमानता ।
ज्ञेयः स परिनिष्पन्नस्वभावोऽनन्यथात्वतः ॥३ ॥
tasya khyātur yathākhyānaṃ yā sadāvidyamānatā|
jñeyaḥ sa pariniṣpannasvabhāvo'nanyathātvataḥ ||3||

तत्र किं ख्यात्यसत्कल्पः कथं ख्याति द्वयात्मना ।
तस्य का नास्तिता तेन या तत्राद्वयधर्मता ॥४ ॥
tatra kiṃ khyāty asatkalpaḥ kathaṃ khyāti dvayātmanā|
tasya kā nāstitā tena yā tatrādvayadharmatā ||4||

Treatise on Three Natures

Translated by Ben Connelly and Weijen Teng

The imaginary, dependent, and
Complete, realized natures:
The wise say these three
Are what is known as profound. ||1||

What appears is the dependent.
How it appears is the imaginary,
Since it is dependent on conditions,
And it exists as mere imagination. ||2||

The constant absence of
How it appears in what appears
Is known as the complete, realized nature,
Since it is never otherwise. ||3||

What appears there? unreal imagination.
How does it appear? as being dual
What is its nonexistence?
The essential nonduality there. ||4||

असत्कल्पोऽत्र कश्चित्तं यतस्तेन हि कल्प्यते ।
यथा च कल्पयत्यर्थ तथात्यन्तं न विद्यते ॥५॥

asatkalpo'tra kaś cittaṃ yatas tena hi kalpyate|
yathā ca kalpayatyartha tathātyantaṃ na vidyate ||5||

तद्धेतुफलभावेन चित्तं द्विविधमिष्यते ।
यदालयाख्यं विज्ञानं प्रवृत्त्याख्यं च सप्तधा ॥६॥

tadd hetuphalabhāvena cittaṃ dvividham iṣyate|
yadālayākhyaṃ vijñānaṃ pravṛttyākhyaṃ ca saptadhā ||6||

संक्लेशवासनाबीजैश्चितत्वाच्चित्तमुच्यते ।
चित्तमाद्यं द्वितीयं तु चित्राकारप्रवृत्तितः ॥७॥

saṃkleśavāsanābījaiś citatvāc cittamucyate|
cittam ādyaṃ dvitīyaṃ tu citrākārapravṛttitaḥ ||7||

समासतोऽभूतकल्पः स चैष त्रिविधो मतः ।
वैपाकिकस्तथा नैमित्तिकोऽन्यः प्रातिभासिकः ॥८॥

samāsato'bhūtakalpaḥ sa caiṣa trividho mataḥ|
vaipākikas tathā naimittiko'nyaḥ prātibhāsikaḥ ||8||

प्रथमो मूलविज्ञानं तद्विपाकात्मकं यतः ।
अन्यः प्रवृत्तिविज्ञानं दृश्यदृग्वित्तिवृत्तितः ॥९॥

prathamo mūlavijñānaṃ tadvipākātmakaṃ yataḥ|
anyaḥ pravṛttivijñānaṃ dṛśyadṛgvittivṛttitaḥ ||9||

What is the unreal imagination there?
Mind. Since it is imagined like this,
Both how it is imagined and the thing imagined
Are ultimately thus, undiscoverable. ||5||

Mind is said to be twofold,
Cause and result,
Also called store consciousness and
Arising consciousness, which is sevenfold. ||6||

First it is called mind (*citta*) because
It is full of (*citatvāt*) seeds of afflictive tendencies.
Second it is called mind (*citta*) because
It is the arising of various (*citra*) appearances. ||7||

In brief, the unreal imagination
Is considered threefold.
Ripening, thus caused,
Or else appearance. ||8||

The first is the root consciousness
For it is characterized by ripening
The others are the arising consciousnesses;
They are the active cognition of seer and seen. ||9||

सदसत्त्वाद् द्वयैकत्वात् संक्लेशव्यवदानयोः ।
लक्षणाभेदतश्चेष्टा स्वभावानां गंभीरता ॥१०॥

sadasattvād dvayaikatvāt saṃkleśavyavadānayoḥ|
lakṣaṇābhedataś ceṣṭā svabhāvānāṃ gambhīratā ||10||

सत्त्वेन गृह्यते यस्मादत्यन्ताभाव एव च ।
स्वभावः कल्पितस्तेन सदसल्लक्षणो मतः ॥११॥

sattvena gṛhyate yasmād atyantābhāva eva ca|
svabhāvaḥ kalpitas tena sadasallakṣaṇo mataḥ ||11||

विद्यते भ्रान्तिभावेन यथाख्यानं न विद्यते ।
परतन्त्रो यतस्तेन सदसल्लक्षणो मतः ॥१२॥

vidyate bhrāntibhāvena yathākhyānaṃ na vidyate|
paratantro yatas tena sadasallakṣaṇo mataḥ ||12||

अद्वयत्वेन यच्चास्ति द्वयस्याभाव एव च ।
स्वभावस्तेन निष्पन्नः सदसल्लक्षणो मतः ॥१३॥

advayatvena yac cāsti dvayasyābhāva eva ca|
svabhāvas tena niṣpannaḥ sadasallakṣaṇo mataḥ ||13||

द्वैविध्यात् कल्पितार्थस्य तदसत्त्वैकभावतः ।
स्वभावः कल्पितो बालैर्द्वयैकत्वात्मको मतः ॥१४॥

dvaividhyāt kalpitārthasya tadasattvaikabhāvataḥ|
svabhāvaḥ kalpito bālair dvayaikatvātmako mataḥ ||14||

Because affliction and cessation are both
Existent and nonexistent, both dual and one,
Not different in characteristics,
These natures are said to be profound. ||10||

Both grasped as existing and really not existing,
The imaginary nature is considered
To have the characteristic
Of existence and nonexistence. ||11||

Since it exists as an illusion, and does not exist
As it appears, the dependent
Is considered to have the characteristic
Of existence and nonexistence. ||12||

Since it exists as nonduality and is the very
Nonexistence of duality, the complete, realized nature
Is considered to have the characteristic
Of existence and nonexistence. ||13||

Since an imagined thing is known as dual
But being one due to the absence of that duality,
The imaginary nature of the foolish
Is said to be both dual and unitary. ||14||

प्रख्यानाद् द्वयभावेन भ्रान्तिमात्रैकभावतः ।
स्वभावः परतन्त्राख्यो द्वयैकत्वात्मको मतः ॥१५॥

prakhyānād dvayabhāvena bhrāntimātraikabhāvataḥ|
svabhāvaḥ paratantrākhyo dvayaikatvātmako mataḥ ||15||

द्वयाभावस्वभावत्वादद्वयैकस्वभावतः ।
स्वभावः परिनिष्पन्नो द्वयैकत्वात्मको मतः ॥१६॥

dvayābhāvasvabhāvatvād advayaikasvabhāvataḥ|
svabhāvaḥ pariniṣpanno dvayaikatvātmako mataḥ ||16||

कल्पितः परतन्त्रश्च ज्ञेयं संक्लेशलक्षणम् ।
परिनिष्पन्न इष्टस्तु व्यवदानस्य लक्षणम् ॥१७॥

kalpitaḥ paratantraśca jñeyaṃ saṃkleśalakṣaṇam|
pariniṣpanna iṣṭas tu vyavadānasya lakṣaṇam ||17||

असद्द्वयस्वभावत्वात् तदभावस्वभावतः ।
स्वभावात् कल्पिताज्ज्ञेयो निष्पन्नोऽभिन्नलक्षणः ॥१८॥

asaddvayasvabhāvatvāt tadabhāvasvabhāvataḥ|
svabhāvāt kalpitājjñeyo niṣpanno'bhinnalakṣaṇaḥ ||18||

अद्वयत्वस्वभावत्वाद् द्वयाभावस्वभावतः ।
निष्पन्नात् कल्पितश्चैव विज्ञेयोऽभिन्नलक्षणः ॥१९॥

advayatvasvabhāvatvād dvayābhāvasvabhāvataḥ|
niṣpannāt kalpitaścaiva vijñeyo'bhinnalakṣaṇaḥ ||19||

Since it appears to have a dual nature,
And being one as that is mere illusion,
The dependent nature
Is said to be both dual and unitary. ||15||

Since it is the nature of dual existence,
And the singular nature of nonduality,
The complete, realized nature
Is said to be both dual and unitary. ||16||

The imaginary and dependent are known
As the characteristic of affliction.
While the complete, realized is known
As the characteristic of purity. ||17||

Due to nonexistent duality nature and
That very nonexistence nature,
The complete, realized is said to be nondifferent
In characteristic from the imaginary. ||18||

Due to nonduality nature and
Nonexistent duality nature,
The imaginary nature is said to be nondifferent
In characteristic from the realized. ||19||

यथाख्यानमसद्भावात् तथासत्त्वस्वभावतः ।
स्वभावात् परतन्त्राख्यान्निष्पन्नोऽभिन्नलक्षणः ॥२०॥

yathākhyānam asadbhāvāt tathāsattvasvabhāvataḥ|
svabhāvāt paratantrākhyān niṣpanno'bhinnalakṣaṇaḥ ||20||

असद्द्वयस्वभावत्वाद् यथाख्यानास्वभावतः ।
निष्पन्नात् परतन्त्रोऽपि विज्ञेयोऽभिन्नलक्षणः ॥२१॥

asaddvayasvabhāvatvād yathākhyānāsvabhāvataḥ|
niṣpannāt paratantro'pi vijñeyo'bhinnalakṣaṇaḥ ||21||

क्रमभेदः स्वभावानां व्यवहाराधिकरतः ।
तत्प्रवेशाधिकाराच्च व्युत्पत्त्यर्थं विधीयते ॥२२॥

kramabhedaḥ svabhāvānāṃ vyavahārādhikārataḥ|
tatpraveśādhikārāc ca vyutpattyarthaṃ vidhīyate ||22||

कल्पितो व्यवहारात्मा व्यवहर्त्रात्मकोऽपरः ।
व्यवहारसमुच्छेदस्वभावश्चान्य इष्यते ॥२३॥

kalpito vyavahārātmā vyavahartrātmako'paraḥ|
vyavahārasamucchedasvabhāvaś cānya iṣyate ||23||

द्वयाभावात्मकः पूर्वं परतन्त्रः प्रविश्यते ।
ततः प्रविश्यते तत्र कल्पमात्रमसद्द्वयम् ॥२४॥

dvayābhāvātmakaḥ pūrvaṃ paratantraḥ praviśyate|
tataḥ praviśyate tatra kalpamātram asaddvayam ||24||

Due to the nonexistence of how it appears,
And being the reality of that very nature,
The realized is said to be nondifferent
In characteristic from the dependent appearance. ||20||

Due to nonexistent duality nature and
Since how it appears is not its own nature,
The dependent is said to be nondifferent
In characteristic from the realized. ||21||

For the purpose of growth in understanding.
These natures are often understood in stages
From the point of view of conventions
and insight into them. ||22||

The imagined is conventional existence,
The other is the maker of conventional existence,
The third nature is the cutting off
Of convention, it is said. ||23||

First one understands the dependent,
A dual nonexistence.
Then one understands the merely imaginary there,
Nonexistent duality. ||24||

ततो द्वयाभावभावो निष्पन्नोऽत्र प्रविश्यते ।
तथा ह्यसावेव तदा अस्तिनास्तीति चोच्यते ॥२५ ॥

tato dvayābhāvabhāvo niṣpanno'tra praviśyate|
tathā hy asāv eva tadā astināstīti cocyate ||25||

त्रयोऽप्येते स्वभावा हि अद्वयालम्बलक्षणाः ।
अभावादतथाभावात् तदभावस्वभावतः ॥२६ ॥

trayo'pyete svabhāvā hi advayālambalakṣaṇāḥ|
abhāvād atathābhāvāt tadabhāvasvabhāvataḥ ||26||

मायाकृतं मन्त्रवशात् ख्याति हस्त्यात्मना यथा ।
आकारमात्रं तत्रास्ति हस्ती नास्ति तु सर्वथा ॥२७ ॥

māyākṛtaṃ mantravaśāt khyāti hastyātmanā yathā|
ākāramātraṃ tatrāsti hastī nāsti tu sarvathā ||27||

स्वभावः कल्पितो हस्ती परतन्त्रस्तदाकृतिः ।
यस्तत्र हस्त्यभावोऽसौ परिनिष्पन्न इष्यते ॥२८ ॥

svabhāvaḥ kalpito hastī paratantras tadākṛtiḥ|
yas tatra hastyabhāvo'sau pariniṣpanna iṣyate ||28||

असत्कल्पस्तथा ख्याति मूलचित्ताद् द्वयात्मना ।
द्वयमत्यन्ततो नास्ति तत्रास्त्याकृतिमात्रकम् ॥२९ ॥

asatkalpas tathā khyāti mūlacittād dvayātmanā|
dvayam atyantato nāsti tatrāsty ākṛtimātrakam ||29||

Then one understands the realized,
The existence of the nonexistence of duality,
For then it is just thus—
It is said to be and not to be. ||25||

The three natures have the characteristic
Of nonduality, ungraspability,
Due to nonexistence, not existing like it appears,
And being the nature of that nonexistence. ||26||

Just as an illusion produced by an incantation
May appear to be an elephant
A mere form is there,
But the elephant is truly no elephant. ||27||

The imaginary nature is the elephant,
Its appearance is the dependent, and
The nonexistence of the elephant there
Is said to be the complete, realized nature. ||28||

The false imagination thus appears
From the root mind as dual.
The duality is utterly nonexistent,
The mere appearance is there. ||29||

मन्त्रवन्मूलविज्ञानं काष्ठवत्तथता मता ।
हस्त्याकारवदेष्टव्यो विकल्पो हस्तिवद् द्वयम् ॥३०॥

mantravan mūlavijñānaṃ kāṣṭhavat tathatā matā|
hastyākāravad eṣṭavyo vikalpo hastivad dvayam ||30||

अर्थतत्त्वप्रतिवेधे युगपल्लक्षणत्रयम् ।
परिज्ञा च प्रहाणं च प्राप्तिश्चेष्टा यथाक्रमम् ॥३१॥

arthatattvaprativedhe yugapal lakṣaṇatrayam|
parijñā ca prahāṇaṃ ca prāptiś ceṣṭā yathākramam ||31||

परिज्ञानुपलम्भोऽत्र हानिरख्यानमिष्यते ।
उपलम्भनिमित्ता तु प्राप्तिः साक्षात्क्रियापि सा ॥३२॥

parijñānupalambho'tra hānirakhyānamiṣyate|
upalambhanimittā tu prāptiḥ sākṣātkriyāpi sā ||32||

द्वयस्यानुपलम्भेन द्वयाकारो विगच्छति ।
विगमात् तस्य निष्पन्नो द्वयाभावोऽधिगम्यते ॥३३॥

dvayasyānupalambhena dvayākāro vigacchati|
vigamāt tasya niṣpanno dvayābhāvo'dhigamyate ||33||

हस्तिनोऽनुपलम्भश्च विगमश्च तदाकृतेः ।
उपलम्भश्च काष्ठस्य मायायां युगपद् यथा ॥३४॥

hastino'nupalambhaś ca vigamaśca tadākṛteḥ|
upalambhaś ca kāṣṭhasya māyāyāṃ yugapad yathā ||34||

The root consciousness is like the mantra,
Thusness is like the wood,
Conceptualization is like the appearance
Of the elephant, and duality is like the elephant. ||30||

In understanding how things really are,
The three characteristics are employed together
Corresponding respectively with knowing,
Relinquishment, and attainment. ||31||

It is said that knowledge is nonperception,
Relinquishment is nonappearance,
Groundless perception though
Is attainment, direct realization. ||32||

Through not perceiving duality,
The dual form vanishes.
Through vanishing, the realized,
Nonduality, is attained. ||33||

Just like with the illusion,
The nonperception of the elephant,
The vanishing of its form, and the perception
Of the piece of wood all occur at once. ||34||

विरुद्धधीवारणत्वाद् बुद्ध्या वैयर्थ्यदर्शनात्।
ज्ञानत्रयानुवृत्तेश्च मोक्षापत्तिरयत्नतः ॥३५॥

viruddhadhīvāraṇatvād buddhyā vaiyarthyadarśanāt|
jñānatrayānuvṛtteśca mokṣāpattirayatnataḥ ||35||

चित्तमात्रोपलम्भेन ज्ञेयार्थानुपलम्भता।
ज्ञेयार्थानुपलम्भेन स्याच्चित्तानुपलम्भता ॥३६॥

cittamātropalambhena jñeyārthānupalambhatā|
jñeyārthānupalambhena syāccittānupalambhatā ||36||

द्वयोरनुपलम्भेन धर्मधातूपलम्भता
धर्मधातूपलम्भेन स्याद् विभुत्वोपलम्भता ॥३७॥

dvayor anupalambhena dharmadhātūpalabhatā|
dharmadhātūpalambhena syād vibhutvopalambhatā ||37||

उपलब्धविभुत्वश्च स्वपरार्थप्रसिद्धितः।
प्राप्नोत्यनुत्तरां बोधिं धीमान् कायत्रयात्मिकाम् ॥३८॥

upalabdhavibhutvaś ca svaparārthaprasiddhitaḥ|
prāpnoty anuttarāṃ bodhiṃ dhīmān kāyatrayātmikām ||38||

इति त्रिस्वभावनिर्देशः समाप्तः॥
कृतिराचार्यवसुबन्धुपादानामिति॥

iti trisvabhāvanirdeśaḥ samāptaḥ
kṛtir ācāryavasubandhupādānām iti

By these reasons—minds cause contrary views,
Minds see unreal things,
Accordance with the three knowledges, and
Effortless attainment of liberation— ||35||

Through the perception of mind-only,
There is no perception of knowable things.
Through the nonperception of knowable things,
There is no perception of mind. ||36||

Through not perceiving either,
The dharma realm is perceived
Through perceiving the dharma realm,
Unlimitedness is perceived. ||37||

Through perceiving unlimitedness,
Accomplishing well-being for self and others,
The wise know unsurpassable awakening,
The threefold body. ||38||

Thus is completed the work
Treatise on Three Natures
Of Venerable Acharya Vasubandhu.

Acknowledgments

Innumerable conditions have supported the creation of this book. I feel gratitude and offer thanks. I cannot name all to whom I'm grateful, but pray you know my heart of appreciation.

Thanks to the many English language scholars of Yogacara who have illumined the way: Karl Brunnhölzl, Jonathan Gold, Dan Lusthaus, Jan Willis, Traleg Kyabgon, Tagawa Shun'ei, Reb Anderson, John Powers, Joy Brennan, William Waldron, Jin Park, Thomas Kochumuttom, Stefan Anacker, Red Pine, Thich Nhat Hanh, and many others. Without the painstaking work of academic scholarship, Buddhism in the English language would be profoundly impoverished.

I thank Weijen Teng for his leap into this work with me, and for his broad scope of knowledge, insight, and precision in translation.

I offer thanks to the Khyentse Foundation for their generous grant to support the creation of this book.

For the blazing suns and sacred nights, the greatest ancestors of Buddhism who have shown the way: the Buddha, Mahapajapati, Bodhidharma, Dogen; and to those Buddhist icons who have touched my heart most personally: Patacara, Shitou, Yikui, Tilopa, Hongzhi; to the thousands across all Buddhist lineages and times who have walked a path of liberation; and to one of my greatest inspirations, Vasubandhu, I offer a bow of gratitude.

To those who have poured their lives into healing and liberation, who have manifested the wisdom of the Mahayana through their very bodies, though a few of them may never have heard a word of Dharma: B. R. Ambedkar, Harriet Tubman, Martin Luther King, Winona LaDuke, bell hooks, Audre Lorde, Malala Yousafzai, Dorothy Day, and so many more. Though these famous folks have inspired me, I know that millions of others whose names I am not singing give so much so that we may all be free. I offer a bow of gratitude for every drop of your vast cleansing rain of love.

To all at Wisdom Publications for your commitment and skill, and especially Marie Scarles, and this book's incomparable editor, Laura Cunningham, for all the carefulness, creativity, and good heart you bring to our work.

To Dainin and Tomoe Katagiri for bringing Zen to Minneapolis and transforming my life; to my teacher, Tim Burkett, for his unflagging support and inspiration; and to my entire beloved Minnesota Zen Meditation Center community. Let me call the names of Kimberly Johnson, Ted O'Toole, Rosemary Taylor,

Bussho Lahn, Susan Nelson, and Guy Gibbon (may he bloom like a flower in the garden of enlightenment). To dear friends at Northside Yoga Room, to the Buddhists from diverse traditions around Twin Cities and the world who have opened their hearts to me, to Pamela Ayo Yetunde, Ven. Thuan Bach, Todd Tsuchiya, Chiemi Onikura Bly, and to so many others, I offer a bow.

To my brothers, sisters, and nonbinary beloved of Multifaith Anti-Racist Change and Healing, Minnesota Multifaith Network, and Minnesota Interfaith Power and Light. I know the work of building love as power amid our differences can be hard, but oh the joy of knowing you! I offer a bow.

To those old friends who are always there when I really need it: Andy, Meleck, Kerith, Benno, Jason, Hippy Johnny, Jesse—I can't name you all, but I send love and thanks.

To the therapists and addiction counselors who have walked with me, I cannot thank you enough. To all the friends of Bill, the Recovery Dharma, and Buddhism and twelve-step folks, that I am alive is your gift to me, and I don't forget it. We are doing this together, and I am grateful.

To my father, Peter, who died twenty years ago, and whose love and radiant mind are alive right here and now, and to my dear mother and brother, Karin and Chris. You have been so good to me. To my children,

Daisy, Delaney, Finn, Max, and Rocky, you have raised me up in the most wonderful ways. To my beloved wife, Colleen, for being exactly who you are, here, in the morning, all the day, and after the sun has fallen.

Notes

1 Easwaran, *The Dhammapada*, 200.

2 See also Connelly, *Inside Vasubandhu's Yogacara*, 158–61.

3 Grant, *Daughters of Emptiness*, 48.

4 Sotoshu Shumucho and the Soto Zen Text Project, *Soto School Scriptures for Daily Services and Practice*, 81.

5 The three quotes in this paragraph are from Hoffman, *The Case Against Reality*, 42, 112, and 114, respectively.

6 Bodhi, *In the Buddha's Words*, 356.

7 Pine, *The Lankavatara Sutra*, 183.

8 Easwaran, *The Dhammapada*, 105.

9 Das, *Heidi Larson*, 877.

10 Samutta Nikaya 22.100. Bodhi, *The Connected Discourses of the Buddha*, 959.

11 Anguttara Nikaya, 10:206. Thera and Bodhi, "The Extinction of Karma," 1.

12 Connelly, *Inside Vasubandhu's Yogacara*, 19.

13 Tanahashi, *Moon in a Dewdrop*, 70.

14 See, for instance, Grouios et al., "The Effect of a Simulated Mental Practice Technique on Free Throw Shooting Accuracy of Highly Skilled Basketball Players."

15 Pine, *The Lankavatara Sutra*, 77.

16 Coseru, *Percieving Reality*, 94.

17 Grant, *Zen Echoes*, 98.

18 Ibid., 139

19 Brunnhölzl, *A Compendium of the Mahayana*, 360.

20 Roberts, *The Mind of Mahamudra*, 72.

21 Ferguson, *Zen's Chinese Heritage*, 300.

22 Yetunde, "Audre Lorde's Hopelessness and Hopefulness."

23 Green, *The Sayings of Layman P'ang*, 15.

24 *Dhammapada* XV. Buddharakkarita, "Sukhavagga: Happiness."

25 Grant, *Daughters of Emptiness,* 75.

26 Ferguson, *Zen's Chinese Heritage,* 156.

27 Tanahashi, *Moon in a Dewdrop,* 70.

28 Nanamoli, *The Path of Purification,* 529.

29 Powers, *Wisdom of the Buddha,* 103.

30 Bodhi, *In the Buddha's Words,* 365.

31 Brunnhölzl, *A Compendium of the Mahayana,* 382.

32 Connelly, *Inside Vasubandhu's Yogacara,* 19.

33 Brunnhölzl, *A Compendium of the Mahayana,* 233.

34 Ibid., 233–34.

35 Ibid., 1374.

36 Ibid., 312.

37 Ibid., 244.

38 Murcott, *The First Buddhist Women,* 116–17.

39 Pine, *The Lankavatara Sutra,* 85.

40 Powers, *Wisdom of Buddha,* 81.

41 Thurman, *The Holy Teaching of Vimalakirti,* 21.

42 Easwaran, *The Dhammapada,* 236 and 205, respectively.

43 Brunnhölzl, *A Compendium of the Mahayana,* 207.

44 Ibid.

45 Cleary, *Entry into the Realm of Reality,* 72.

46 Leighton, *Cultivating the Empty Field,* 41.

47 Caplow and Moon, *The Hidden Lamp,* 271.

48 Watson, "The Diamond Sutra."

49 Samyutta Nikaya 22.95. Bodhi, *The Connected Discourses of the Buddha,* 952.

50 Thurman, *Holy Teachings of Vimalakirti,* 61.

51 Tanahashi, *Moon in a Dewdrop,* 134–38.

52 Anguttara Nikaya, 10:206. Thera and Bodhi, "The Extinction of Karma," 1.

53 Samyutta Nikaya 56.11. Thanissaro, "Dhammacakkappavattana Sutta."

54 Bodhi, *In the Buddha's Words,* 366.

55 Tarrant, *Bring Me the Rhinoceros,* 49.

56 Caplow and Moon, *The Hidden Lamp,* 48.

57 Grant, *Daughters of Emptiness,* 38.

58 Roberts, *The Mind of Mahamudra,* 190.

59   Brunnhölzl, *Compendium of the Mahayana*, 184–85.
60   Tanahashi, *Moon in a Dewdrop*, 102.
61   Easwaran, *The Dhammapada*, 105.
62   Brunnhölzl, *A Compendium of the Mahayana*, 207.
63   Levering, "Zen for the Women's Quarters," 5.
64   Watson, "The Diamond Sutra."
65   Samyutta Nikaya 22:87. Bodhi, *The Connected Discourses of the Buddha*, 939.
66   Grant, *Daughters of Emptiness*, 29.
67   Thanissaro, "Rohitassa Sutta."
68   Roberts, *The Mind of Mahamudra*, 76.

Selected Bibliography

Anacker, Stefan. *Seven Works of Vasubandhu*. Delhi: Motilal Bandarsidass, 1984.

Anderson, Reb. *The Third Turning of the Wheel*. Berkeley: Rodmell Press, 2012.

Bodhi, Bhikku. *In the Buddha's Words*. Boston: Wisdom Publications, 2005.

Bodhi, Bhikku. *The Connected Discourses of the Buddha*. Somerville, MA: Wisdom Publications, 2000.

Brunnhölzl, Karl. *A Compendium of the Mahayana*. Boulder, CO: Snow Lion, 2018.

Buddharakkhita, Acharya, trans. "Sukhavagga: Happiness." *Access to Insight (BCBS Edition)*, 30 November 2013. http://www.accesstoinsight.org/tipitaka/kn/dhp/dhp.15.budd.html .

Caplow, Florence, and Susan Moon. *The Hidden Lamp*. Somerville, MA: Wisdom Publications, 2013.

Cleary, Thomas. *Buddhist Yoga*. Boston: Shambhala Publications, 1995.

Cleary, Thomas. *Entry into the Realm of Reality*. Boston: Shambhala Publications, 1987.

Connelly, Ben. *Inside Vasubandhu's Yogacara*. Somerville, MA: Wisdom Publications, 2016.

Coseru, Christian. *Perceiving Reality*. New York, NY: Oxford University Press, 2012.

Das, Pamela. "Heidi Larson: Shifting the Conversation About Vaccine Confidence." *The Lancet* 396, no. 10255 (September 26, 2020): 877. doi:10.1016/S0140-6736(20)31612-3.

Easwaran, Eknath, trans. *The Dhammapada*. Tomales, CA: Nilgiri Press, 2007.

Ferguson, Andy. *Zen's Chinese Heritage*. Somerville, MA: Wisdom Publications, 2011.

Gold, Jonathan. *Paving the Great Way*. New York, NY: Columbia Univ. Press, 2015.

Grant, Beata. *Daughters of Emptiness*. Somerville, MA: Wisdom Publications, 2003.

———. *Zen Echoes*. Somerville, MA: Wisdom Publications, 2017.

Green, James. *The Sayings of Layman P'ang*. Boston: Shambhala Publications, 2009.

Grouios, George, Klio Semoglou, Konstantinos Chatzinikolaou, Katerina Mousikou, and Christos Kabitsis. "The Effect of a Simulated Mental Practice Technique on Free Throw Shooting Accuracy of Highly Skilled Basketball Players." *Journal of Human Movement Studies* 33, no. 3 (January 1997): 119–38.

Hanh, Thich Nhat. *Buddha Mind, Buddha Body*. Berkeley: Parallax, 2007.

Hanh, Thich Nhat. *Understanding Our Mind*. Berkeley: Parallax, 2006.

Hoffman, Donald. *The Case Against Reality*. New York, NY: W.W. Norton & Company, 2019.

Jacobs, Beth. *The Original Buddhist Psychology*. Berkeley: North Atlantic Books, 2017.

Khenpo Shenga and Ju Mipham, *Middle Beyond Extremes*. Ithaca, NY: Snow Lion, 2006.

Kochumuttom, Thomas. *A Buddhist Doctrine of Experience*. Delhi: Motilal Bandarsidass, 1982.

Leighton, Taigen Dan. *Cultivating the Empty Field*. North Clarendon, VT: Tuttle, 2000.

Levering, Miriam. "Zen for the Women's Quarters: The Teachings of Soshin-ni." Paper presented to the American Academy of Religion Conference, November 21–23, 2004, San Antonio.

Lusthaus, Dan. *Buddhist Phenomenology*. New York: RoutledgeCurzon, 1992.

Murcott, Susan. *The First Buddhist Women*. Berkeley: Parallax, 1991.

Nanamoli, Bhikku, trans. *The Path of Purification* (*Visuddhimagga*). By Bhadantacariya Buddhaghosa. Kandy, Sri Lanka: Buddhist Publication Society, 2010. Pdf e-book. https://www.accesstoinsight.org/lib/authors/nanamoli/PathofPurification2011.pdf.

Pine, Red, trans. *The Lankavatara Sutra*. Berkeley: Counterpoint, 2012.

Powers, John, *Wisdom of the Buddha*. Berkeley, CA: Dharma Publishing, 1995.

Rinbochay, Lati. *Mind in Tibetan Buddhism*. Valois, NY: Snow Lion, 1980.

Roberts, Peter Allen. *The Mind of Mahamudra*. Somerville, MA: Wisdom Publications, 2014.

Schireson, Grace. *Zen Women*. Somerville, MA: Wisdom Publications, 2009.

Shun'ei, Tagawa. *Living Yogacara*. Boston: Wisdom Publications, 2009.

Sotoshu Shumucho and the Soto Zen Text Project. *Soto School Scriptures for Daily Services and Practice*. Tokyo: Sotoshu Shumucho, 2001. Pdf e-book.

Tanahashi, Kazuaki. *Moon in a Dewdrop: Writings of Zen Master Dogen*. New York, NY: North Point Press, 1985.

Tarrant, John. *Bring Me the Rhinoceros: And Other Zen Koans That Will Save Your Life*. Boston: Shambhala Publications, 2008.

Thanissaro Bhikkhu, trans. "Dhammacakkappavattana Sutta: Setting the Wheel of Dhamma in Motion" (SN 56.11). *Access to Insight (BCBS Edition)*, 30 November 2013. http://www.accesstoinsight.org/tipitaka/sn/sn56/sn56.011.than.html.

———. "Rohitassa Sutta: To Rohitassa" (AN 4.45). Access to Insight (BCBS Edition), 30 November 2013. http://www.accesstoinsight.org/tipitaka/an/an04/an04.045.than.html.

Thera, Nyanaponika and Bhikkhu Bodhi, trans. "The Extinction of Karma." *The Wheel*, no. 241–42. Kandy, Sri Lanka: Buddhist Publication Society, 1970. Pdf e-book, 1990. http://insights-into-karma.org/past-karma/the-extinction-of-karma.

Thurman, Robert. *The Holy Teaching of Vimalakirti*. University Park, PA, Pennsylvania State University Press, 1976.

Waldron, William, *The Buddhist Unconscious*, Abingdon, UK: Routledge, 2003.

Watson, Burton. "The Diamond Sutra." *The Eastern Buddhist* 41, no. 1 (2010): 67–100. http://www.jstor.org/stable/26289589.

Willis, Jan. *On Knowing Reality*. New York, NY: Columbia Univ. Press, 1979.

Yetunde, Pamela Ayo. "Audre Lorde's Hopelessness and Hopefulness: Cultivating a Womanist Nondualism for Psycho-Spiritual Wholeness." Feminist Theology 27, no. 2, 176–94.

Index

root of, xvii, 132

stages of development in, 140

women in, 175–76

See also Early Buddhism; East Asian Buddhism; Engaged Buddhism; Mahayana Buddhism; Tibetan Buddhism

Burkett, Tim, 38, 231

C

Caodong Chan, 104

Carson, Rachel, 127–28

caste system, 144

Catholicism, 143

cause and effect/result, 37–39, 44–45, 48, 59–64, 237. *See also* karma

certainty, 57, 163

cessation, 69, 70, 109, 192, 237, 239

Chan tradition, xi, 65, 66, 97, 104, 138, 202–3

characteristic (*laksana*), uses of term, 109–11

Chicago, Judy, 191

childhood experiences, 181

cognitive science, viii

compassion, 112, 116, 122, 165, 231

with afflictions, 119

delusion about, 197

dependent nature and, 7–8

developing, 140, 169

and emptiness, relationship between, 196

impact of, 66

natural, 1

for oneself, 183

in science, 63

seeds of, 47

See also under awareness

compassionate action, 55, 102

complete, realized nature, 8–10, 17, 113, 138, 207, 235

absolute truth and, 38, 72–73

attaining, 190, 192, 193

as cutting off convention, 143, 146–48, 243

dependent nature and, 125–29, 131–35, 223–24, 241, 243

as dharmakaya, 230

as dual and unitary, 103, 105–7, 241

existence and nonexistence of, 87, 90, 239

imaginary nature and, 17–18, 19, 115–20, 121, 122–24, 241

as "never otherwise," 19–22

as nirvana, 111–12

positive aspect of, 186

as purity, 109, 241

as right here, 218, 226–27

as thusness, 189

translations of term, 18

understanding, 155, 243

concepts and conceptualization, 127–28, 145, 185, 187

conditioning

afflictive tendencies from, 45

appearances and, 127

exhausting, 47

facts and, 27–28

Dharma, 162
  harmony with, 146–47
  and its meaning, inseparability
    of, 163
  preached by inanimate things,
    104
  realm (*dharmadhatu*), 223,
    224–26, 227, 249
  women teachers of, 176
dharmakaya, 230–31
Dharmakirti, 62
dharmas, 33–34, 162–63, 215
dharmata, 24, 26, 132, 215
dhatu, uses of term, 225–26
Diamond Sutra, 137, 138, 162–63,
  221
Dignaga, 28, 122
Dogen Zenji, 20, 55, 110, 120,
  127, 176–77, 213
Dongshan, 103–4
dreams, 16, 17–18, 60, 213–14
duality, 2–3, 29, 93–96, 239
  of cause and result, 37
  compassion and, 197
  existence of nonexistence of,
    155, 156, 243
  as illusory, 187
  importance of, 23
  mind's role in, 35
  nonappearance of, 206
  nonexistent nature of, 121,
    131–33, 179, 184, 241, 243,
    245
  nonperception of, 201–2, 247
  seeing through, 183
  of sensations, 31–32

  suffering from, 32
  unconscious manifesting of,
    126–27
  working with, 24–27

E

Early Buddhism, x, xiv, xv–xvi
  arhats in, 215
  core teaching of, 9
  identitylessness in, 149–50,
    151
  monastic conduct in, 146
  realms of existence in, 212
  on suffering, 197
  three marks in, 110–11
Earth, 140–41, 144, 145
Earth Day event, 164–65
East Asian Buddhism, 73. *See
  also* Huayan school; Jodo
  Shinshu (Pure Land); Zen
  tradition
ego, 22
eight consciousnesses, 38, 54,
  59–60, 74
eightfold path, xiv, 193
Einstein, Albert, 56, 63
emotions/afflictive emotions, 3
  as barrier, xv–xvi
  dependent arising of, 129
  lessening reactivity to, 119
  mental activity co-arising
    with, 47–48
  mindfulness of, xiv–xv,
    46–48, 88–89, 128–29, 183,
    197, 208
  as mind-only, 35

compassion and, 197
dual, 77–78
emotions and, 128
groundless, 195, 198–200, 247
habits of, 180, 185
as illusory, 167–71
as mind, 36
of mind-only, 217, 218–20,
249
purifying, 139–40
perfectionism, 181
phenomena
identitylessness of, 116–17
as imaginations, 54
as magic show, xvi
tathagata heart of all, 123
physics, theoretical, 21
"Plum Blossom Nun," 226
poetry, 13–14
"Poetry Is Not a Luxury"
(Lorde), 48
post-traumatic stress disorder,
170–71, 179–80, 182–84
projection only, 211–13, 215–16,
218–19. *See also* mind-only
provisional nature, xii, 73
psychology, viii, 74
Buddhist, x, xv–xvi, 39–40
cognitive, 170
purity, 109, 123, 241

R
race and racism, 4–5, 21, 74,
87–89, 116, 181, 231
realms of existence, 212
rebirth, 156, 212

refuge, 189
relative truth. *See* conventional/
relative truth
relaxation, importance of, 78,
80–81
relinquishment, 189, 190, 192,
193, 195, 197, 247
right view, 25, 155
Rohitassa Sutta, 230
Roper, Megan Phelps, 198

S
samatha (calm abiding), xv, 131,
218
samboghakaya, 230
Samdhinirmocana Sutra, 111, 144–
45, 168
samsara
imaginary nature and, 176
mind as source, 44
and nirvana, unity of, 70, 115,
116, 117, 120
nirvana in, 72
as peace, 133
suffering of, 69
Satipatthana Sutta, xiv, 55, 128, 132
Schireson, Grace, 219
Schrödinger, Erwin, 20
science, viii, 63, 169–70, 205
seeds, karmic, 6
accumulations of, 206
fruit, timing of, 49–51, 65–67
fruit of, 46, 180, 181, 182–83
positive, planting, 65, 80, 208
storehouse consciousness and,
38–39, 43, 237

About the Author and Translator

BEN CONNELLY is a Soto Zen teacher and Dharma heir in the Katagiri lineage. He also teaches mindfulness in a wide variety of secular contexts, including police training and addiction recovery groups, and works with multifaith communities focused on intersectional liberation, climate justice, and racial justice. Ben is based at Minnesota Zen Meditation Center and travels to teach across the United States. He's the author of *Inside the Grass Hut: Living Shitou's Classic Zen Poem*, *Inside Vasubandhu's Yogacara: A Practitioner's Guide*, and *Mindfulness and Intimacy.*

WEIJEN TENG is chair of the Department of Buddhist Studies at Dharma Drum Institute of Liberal Arts, Taiwan. He completed his BA degree in Pali and Theravada Buddhism at the University of Kelaniya, Sri Lanka, and his MA in Sanskrit at the University of Poona, India. He enrolled in an MA program in

Religious Studies at the University of Chicago and received his PhD in Religious Studies at Harvard University. Dr. Teng's research interests include the Buddhist theory of mind and meditation, the intellectual history of Chinese Buddhism, and more recently Buddhism and modernity.

What to Read Next
from Wisdom Publications

INSIDE VASUBANDHU'S YOGACARA
A Practitioner's Guide
Ben Connelly
Foreword by Norman Fischer

"Through Connelly's luminous teaching, some of Yogacara's most vivid and inspiring innovations come to life . . . Newcomers and adherents to this lesser-known Buddhist school alike are lucky to have Connelly as an exceptional guide to the central themes of Yogacara."—*Publishers Weekly* Starred Review

INSIDE THE GRASS HUT
Living Shitou's Classic Zen Poem
Ben Connelly
Foreword by Taigen Dan Leighton

"The very essence of Zen."—Mike O'Connor

MINDFULNESS AND INTIMACY
Ben Connelly

"This book carries vital medicine for today's world. Ben Connelly speaks from the heart of Zen and reminds us of our true and innate capacity for intimacy . . . I recommend it for everyone!"
—Deborah Edden Tull, author of *Relational Mindfulness*

LIVING YOGACARA
An Introduction to Consciousness-Only Buddhism
Tagawa Shun'ei
Translated and Introduced by Charles Muller

"This book, expertly translated by Charles Muller, is exceptional for making an extremely complex tradition accessible to the general reader."—*Buddhadharma*

About Wisdom Publications

Wisdom Publications is the leading publisher of classic and contemporary Buddhist books and practical works on mindfulness. To learn more about us or to explore our other books, please visit our website at wisdomexperience.org or contact us at the address below.

Wisdom Publications
199 Elm Street
Somerville, MA 02144 USA

We are a 501(c)(3) organization, and donations in support of our mission are tax deductible.

Wisdom Publications is affiliated with the Foundation for the Preservation of the Mahayana Tradition (FPMT).